DATE			
APR 23 '81			

About the Series

IDEAS IN PROGRESS is a commercially published series of working papers dealing with alternatives to industrial society. It is our belief that the ills and profound frustrations which have overtaken man are not merely due to industrial civilization's inadequate planning and faulty execution, but are caused by fundamental errors in our basic thinking about goals. This series is designed to question and rethink the underlying concepts of many of our institutions and to propose alternatives. Unless this is done soon society will undoubtedly create even greater injustices and inequalities than at present. It is to correct this trend that authors are invited to submit short texts of work in progress of interest not only to their colleagues but also to the general public. The series fosters direct contact between the author and the reader. It provides the author with the opportunity to give wide circulation to his draft while he is still developing an idea. It offers the reader an opportunity to participate critically in shaping this idea before it has taken on a definitive form.

Readers are invited to write directly to the author of the present volume at the following address:

Professor Henryk Skolimowski
College of Engineering
Department of Humanities
The University of Michigan
1079 East Engineering Building
Ann Arbor
Michigan 48109
USA

THE PUBLISHERS

IDEAS IN PROGRESS

ECO-PHILOSOPHY

DESIGNING NEW TACTICS FOR LIVING

Henryk Skolimowski

MARION BOYARS · BOSTON · LONDON

Published simultaneously in Great Britain
and the United States 1981
by Marion Boyars Publishers Ltd.
18 Brewer Street, London W1R 4AS
and Marion Boyars Inc.
99 Main Street, Salem, New Hampshire 03079.

Australian distribution by Thomas C. Lothian
4-12 Tattersalls Lane, Melbourne, Victoria 3000.

British Library Cataloguing in Publication Data
Skolimowski, Henryk
Ecophilosophy. – (Ideas in progress).
1. Civilization
I. Title   II. Series
909   CB68   79-56846

ISBN 0-7145-2677-0 Cloth edition
ISBN 0-7145-2676-2 Paperback edition
Library of Congress Catalog Card Number 79-56846

Set in Monotype Baskerville by Gloucester Typesetting Co Ltd.
Printed and bound by
The Maple-Vail Book Manufacturing Group USA

Contents

Preface

After all the juggling with economic figures is done, there is still life to be lived. The meaning of life is not to be derived from any economic calculations: its roots lie far beyond all economic and physical parameters. Bertrand Russell and other positivists of the 20th century have nearly persuaded us that the human project is to explore the physical world. Eco-philosophy insists that the human project is a re-discovery of human meaning, related to the meaning of the universe.

In exploring the physical world we have created complicated matrices onto which we map the welter of physical phenomena. The complexity of these matrices has become so subtle, complex and exhaustive that we simply have no room for understanding other things, such as human meaning.

One aim of this book is to unravel the variety of mechanistic and physical relationships (within which we are wrapped and by which we are defined) in order to demonstrate that most of our crises, particularly the economic ones, do not arise as the result of mismanagement, ill will or the insufficiency of rationality in our approaches, but arise for more fundamental reasons: they arise because we have constructed a deficient code for reading nature, leading to a deficiency in interacting with nature. The root cause lies in the very foundations of our scientific world view; and in the very perceptions which this world view engenders.

Alternative life styles do not require living differently but also *knowing* differently. We must be able to provide a *rational* justification for our new life styles, which will amount to nothing less than providing a new rationality. We must be convinced in our hearts *and* minds that our frugality is not a depressing abnegation and self-denial but an act of positive manifestation of new qualities; only then will it become *elegant frugality*. Therefore, alternative life styles must signify not only changes in our technology, economics and patterns of living, but changes in our morality, rationality, and conceptual thinking.

On the philosophical level this book attempts to provide the rudiments of a cosmology which consists of a new reading of the furniture of the cosmos. We are positing a new conception of human values and a radical redefinition of the meaning of human life. We propose a new interpretation of evolution. All these elements are woven together into one structure and shown to be integral parts of a new whole which I call *Ecological Humanism*. The overall aim is not only to provide a new philosophy but, above all, to provide a new purpose, a new inspiration and a new hope for mankind; to pave the way for new tactics for living.

Some readers may worry about *how to implement* the program here outlined. My answer is: let us first get our thinking straight, for without that no implementation is possible. Logos is a very subtle and all-pervading form of praxis.

Henryk Skolimowski

I

Knowledge and Values

LET us begin with certain distinctions that are fundamental to the scientific world view and are at the same time responsible for many of our present problems, conceptual and otherwise. One is the distinction between knowledge and values. The separation of these two was a momentous event in the intellectual history of the West, leading as it did to the emancipation of specialized scientific disciplines from the body of natural philosophy. But it was a perilous event, too, in that it led in the long run to a conception of the universe as a clock-like mechanism and to the gradual elimination of such elements of our knowledge as disagreed with that mechanistic view – including intrinsic values, which were replaced by instrumental values.

Logically there would seem to have been two different processes involved: intense exploration of the physical world on the one hand and the slow disappearance of intrinsic human values on the other. This logical separation is misleading, however, for what we have here is not two different processes but two aspects of the same process. The quest for scientific explanations and the growth in importance of the physical sciences coincided with, indeed took place in the context of a decline in the importance of intrinsic values. Our vast store of knowledge of the physical world can thus be said to have been accumulated at the expense of human values. This is a large claim and the present chapter will attempt to justify it. Also in this chapter I shall argue that there appears to be a see-saw relationship between factual knowledge and intrinsic human values: as one goes up, the other is pushed down. If this perception is correct, then it would follow that the resurrection of intrinsic values and their reinstatement at the center of our lives may indeed come about but that it will be at the expense of our adulation of science and of the physical fact, which we have exaggeratedly elevated to the status of deities.

1 *Basic Historical Positions*

Historically we can distinguish at least four basic positions regarding the relation of values to knowledge.

The first is the position of classical antiquity as exemplified by Plato: values and knowledge are fused together; one does not become dominant or subservient to the other. As we know, Plato believed in the unity of truth, goodness and beauty. Within his universe values and knowledge are two aspects of the same thing; no knowledge is value-free, and no values can be regarded as void of knowledge. According to Plato, to possess superior knowledge is to lead a superior life. Knowledge is a vital part of the network of life. Most sins are the fruit of ignorance.

In the Middle Ages we can distinguish a second position: knowledge is fused with values, but at the same time it is subordinated to values which are determined by the Church. Knowledge is in the service of values and must agree with values that are accepted *a priori* as supreme. To grasp God's design, God's order, and the values that follow from that order sometimes required faculties stronger than the mere human intellect, which at times saw discrepancies between natural reason and God's order. Hence revelation was accepted as a mode of cognition, for it allowed one to transcend reason and to find a justification for the fusion of knowledge and values under the supremacy of values.

The remaining two positions can be clearly discerned in the post-Renaissance period. The third position separates knowledge from values, without, however, giving supremacy to either. This position is perhaps best represented by Immanuel Kant (1720–1804), who clearly saw in Newtonian physics indubitable knowledge governing the behavior of the physical universe – a separate realm unto itself; but who, at the same time, would not subject the autonomy and sovereignty of man to any deterministic set of physical laws. Hence he summarized the autonomy of both realms by declaring: 'The starry heavens above you and the moral law within.'

The fourth position is, of course, the one held by classical empiricism and its more recent extensions: nineteenth-century Positivism and twentieth-century Logical Empiricism. This position separates values from knowledge and, by attaching supreme importance to knowledge of things physical and by ruling that values are not proper knowledge, it *ipso facto* establishes the primacy of knowledge over values. This tradition is so near to us and envelops us so constantly and consistently that we are often unable to see through it in order to assess its impact on us.

Thus the four basic positions are: Plato – the fusion of knowledge with values without asserting the primacy of one over the other; Christianity – fusion of the two but asserting the primacy of values; Kant – separation of the two without censure of either; empiricism – the separation of values from knowledge while asserting the primacy of (factual) knowledge over values.

It is, of course, the empiricist position, or the empiricist tradition, that we want to examine in some detail, for this is the tradition that looms largest on our intellectual horizon; this is the tradition that has become our intellectual orthodoxy, the tradition that has been programmed into our ways of thinking and judging, the tradition that has brought the value-vacuum to our society, to our universities, to our individual lives.

The life of cultures and societies is an exceedingly complex affair. What we must do is to unravel the multitude of causes and effects and then see how the original visions and insights of Bacon, Galileo, Descartes, etc. have given rise to larger doctrines, been channelled into various tributaries of learning and life, and been reinforced in the process; and how the process continues to feed upon itself by outlining the boundaries of its territory and maintaining rigid control over what is legitimate within the territory and what is illegitimate. To give two specific examples: research into chemical warfare is 'legitimate', for it is an extension of 'objective knowledge' into the sphere of 'certain chemicals'; research into acupuncture is 'illegitimate', because the phenomenon itself seems to undermine certain fundamental tenets of the empiricist world view. The connection between a particular phenomenon, or a particular strategy, and the basic tenets of the world view is indirect and is usually several steps removed, but it is there, if we have the patience and perseverance to look for it.

Strange as it may seem, this connection is often more readily grasped by intellectually 'unsophisticated', rebellious youth than by the 'sophisticated' minds that govern present-day academia. It is remarkable that, on the basis of some inner moral feedback, young people can sometimes react with strong moral revulsion and complete moral conviction to abuses of knowledge in academia and elsewhere, while academia itself often seems oblivious to those abuses.

The intellectual tradition which has directly and indirectly caused the value-vacuum has its roots in the seventeenth century, during which time the doctrines of Bacon, Descartes, Galileo, Newton, Hobbes, Locke, Hume and others were remolding the world, or rather our picture of it, to make it independent of religion. In the eighteenth century the center of gravity moved to France, where d'Alembert, Condillac,

Condorcet, Diderot, Voltaire, Laplace, La Mettrie and others furthered the cause of secularism and of the scientific world view. Then in the nineteenth century the tradition was continued by Auguste Comte in France, Jeremy Bentham and John Stuart Mill in Britain, and by the leading materialists: Feuerbach, Marx, Engels and Lenin. In the twentieth century the tradition was further articulated, refined, and couched in more sophisticated language by Bertrand Russell in Britain and by the logical empiricists of the Vienna Circle.

More recently this tradition has found its extension in analytical philosophy,[1] in behaviorist psychology, in operationalized social science, in quantity-ridden and computer-obsessed political science, and in quite a variety of other disciplines, which are full of Facts and Figures even if those Facts and Figures explain precious little.

I have sketched the line from Francis Bacon to B. F. Skinner as if it were one uninterrupted, homogeneous development, as if the present predicament were the result of some inexorable logical process. The process was far from homogeneous. What is really startling is the fact that, in spite of a great variety of opposing intellectual forces, the scientific-empiricist world view has prevailed so remarkably.

Parallel to the prevalent empiricist tradition there ran, and still does run, the other tradition, which for lack of a better term we shall call anti-empiricist. This tradition was represented by minds at least as powerful and superlative as those on the empiricist side: Pascal, Leibniz and Spinoza in the seventeenth century, Rousseau and Kant in the eighteenth century, Hegel and Nietzsche in the nineteenth century were all seeking a world liberated from the constraints of scholastic theology, but which was not reducible to quantity and measurement.

Pascal's case is particularly illuminating, for he, more clearly than perhaps anyone else in the seventeenth century, saw the great value and the great attraction of science and, at the same time, the great danger in unconditional sub-mission to science. He wrote: 'Knowledge of physical science will not console me for ignorance of morality in time of affliction, but knowledge of morality will always console me for ignorance of physical science.' (*Pensées*, 23).

Equally illuminating is Spinoza's case. His *Ethics – Demonstrated in the Geometric Order* is the work in which he argues that the good is everything which furthers knowledge, and *vice versa*. Happiness consists solely in knowledge. Virtue itself is knowledge. 'Happiness is not a reward for virtue, but virtue itself.' He further argues that love can be conceived as the perfectibility of man through knowledge, for knowledge induces love – a position not far removed from Plato's. What is most curious about Spinoza's *Ethics* is that it attempts to prove its propositions as if it were a textbook of geometry. Though departing radically from the scientific tradition which was later to prevail, Spinoza paid lip service to it (and more than that) in attempting to provide geometrical (scien-tific?) demonstrations of his ethical convictions.

In the eighteenth century Rousseau and Kant defended, in their respective ways, the autonomy of the human world against the encroachment of the mechanistic world view and the spreading wave of empiricism. Of the two, Rousseau was the flamboyant one, while Kant was the incisive one. Rous-seau eloquently, and sometimes dramatically, protested against 'civilization', which he thought estranged man from his essence and from his fellow men. The 'artificial' ways that civilization imposes on us are at the source of individual and social alienation. This was a prelude to twentieth-century outcries against science and technology for imposing on us their artificial ways.

Kant, on the other hand, held that if empiricism is correct, we possess no certain knowledge of the physical world; if we do possess such knowledge, in the laws of physics, then em-piricism (which insists that the sources of this indubitable knowledge are the senses) collapses. Kant felt compelled to conclude that knowledge of physics provides only a knowledge of the appearances of things, not of 'things-in-themselves'. Kant held, at the same time, that morality is under the complete sovereignty of the human being and is subject to the categorical imperative: 'Act according to the principle which you would like to become the universal law', which applies universally to all human beings. Knowledge of the moral law is not derivable from knowledge of the physical world; it is peculiar to man's understanding of his place in the universe and of his 'duty'.

Both Rousseau and Kant created systems which worked against the homogenization of the world carried on under the auspices of empiricism. They both stood up unflinchingly to the challenge of empiricism. Theirs were imaginative and constructive systems, not merely defensive responses to empiricism. The situation changed in the nineteenth century. Then protest against spreading materialism and positivism was almost invariably expressed from defensive positions – often from the position of despair, as in Nietzsche and some late nineteenth-century poets.

The empiricist tradition, and the entire world view it has brought with itself, was not something inevitable and inexorable. It was one particular intellectual 'strain', which prevailed over other traditions. Those other traditions are still alive; in particular, the conviction of the unity of knowledge and values was maintained in the eighteenth, nineteenth and twentieth centuries (particularly among poets). In protesting against the pernicious pitfalls of empiricism and its offshoots, such as logical positivism, we are not wolves howling in the wilderness, but heirs of a long and great intellectual tradition.

2 *The Eclipse of Values in the Nineteenth Century*

Although the advances of natural science in the seventeenth century were enormous, traditional values still prevailed. Newton himself wrote the *Philosophiae Naturalis Principia Mathematica* to attest to the greatness, glory and perfection of God. Admittedly, empiricists like Locke and Hume were already at work postulating the separation of knowledge from values.

The eighteenth century brought about the transition. The slogans of the French enlightenment were both liberating (from the tethers of the antiquated religious world view) and at the same time ominously constraining for they paved the way to vulgar materialism, shallow positivism and the annihilation of values in the nineteenth century.

The nineteenth century marks the triumph of science and technology and an unprecedented expansion of the scientific world view. The aggressive assertion of positivism and materialism, of which Marxism was a part; of scientific rationality and technological efficiency; of the age of industrialization, which, alas, turned out to be the age of environmental devastation, all pointed towards a brave new world in which traditional (intrinsic) values were consigned to limbo. We need to examine this process more closely in order to understand why the triumphs of science had to signify an eclipse of values.

Science did not develop in a social vacuum but as part of the unfolding new culture. The battle against petrified aspects of institutionalized religion was waged in the seventeenth and eighteenth centuries with almost the same intensity as in the nineteenth century, which was more aggressive and successful in containing the influence of religion in the realm of thought than was true of the previous two centuries. The secular, rational, science-based world view took its place firmly on the stage. The rest seemed merely a matter of

implementation. The time appeared to be near when paradise on earth would prevail.

The battle between science and religion was by no means
confined to purely intellectual matters, to ways of interpret-
ing the world around us. It was also an ideological battle; and
it was an eschatological battle, for what was at stake were the
'ends' of man's life. Religion represented the status quo, it
was turned inward, it urged man to perfect himself, and to
seek the ultimate reward in the after-life. Science represented
a continuous process of change; it was turned outward, and
it promised salvation here on earth. In this battle religion
was often in an alliance with intrinsic values, supported them
and was supported by them. On the other hand, science was
in an alliance with progress. The corollaries of the two opposing forces of religion and science – intrinsic values on the one
hand, and progress on the other – were themselves construed
as adversaries. Indeed 'progressive' and 'revolutionary' individuals in the nineteenth century debunked with equal vehe-
mence both traditional religion and traditional values, which
they somehow identified with the feudal and bourgeois ethos,
regarding them as unworthy of the new epoch, in which
toughness, rationality and a no-nonsense pragmatic attitude
were called for.

In this climate intrinsic values were increasingly dismissed
as vestiges of an obsolete world. It is therefore no wonder that
new doctrines concerning values attempted, implicitly or
explicitly, to serve the scientific world view and to justify its
supremacy. The doctrine of utilitarianism proclaimed that
the cornerstone of our ethics and our actions should be the
principle of the greatest good for the greatest number. Formulated in this way utilitarianism does not seem to signify the
submission of ethics to the dictates of science. However, the
principle was soon vulgarized to mean: the greatest quantity
of material goods for the largest possible number of people.
This is indeed the underlying ethos of the technological or

consumer society. Thus we can see that utilitarianism has become an adjunct to material progress, its ethical justification; material progress itself is an essential part of the scientific-technological world view. A scrupulous historian might object that this interpretation does violence to the original meaning of utilitarianism, as expounded by Jeremy Bentham and John Stuart Mill. Ethical doctrines are judged by what becomes of them in practice. The ease with which utilitarianism was 'instrumentalized' and integrated into the technological society only shows how much it was attuned to the increasingly homogenized 'brave new world'. After all, Bentham and Mill were nineteenth-century empiricists *par excellence*. Their views embodied all the typically empiricist limitations.

Nihilism and scientism, on the other hand, overtly preached the gospel of Science, enshrined Facts as deities, and condemned all products of the human spirit as 'meaningless' or reactionary. One of the most striking expressions of this new tough-mindedness is Sergei Bazarov, as drawn by Turgenev in his novel *Fathers and Sons*. Bazarov, as we remember, is a robust, exuberant and enthusiastic believer in science, in materialism, and in the world in which Facts and Positive Knowledge are supreme values. He has no use for art, for poetry, for other 'romantic rubbish'. Bazarov announces:

' "We have decided merely to deny everything."
' "And this you call nihilism?"
' "That we call nihilism."
' "Like those artists," said Bazarov, "I consider Raphael to be worth not a copper groat. And for the artists themselves, I appreciate them at about a similar sum." '

Bazarov is a comprehensive embodiment of the prevailing nihilism, materialism, scientism and positivism which, in their respective ways, regarded intrinsic values as secondary, insignificant, or even non-existent in the world of cold facts, clinical objectivity and scientific reason.

Now, it takes only a moment's reflection to realize that Bazarov's philosophy has won the day, that big corporations are an incarnation of this philosophy. *Bazarovism*, if I may coin the term, has become the dominant, if only implicit philosophy of the technological society – East and West. It requires one sober look to be aware that the Soviet Union is as much dominated by the Bazarovs as is this society. The mania for continuous economic growth (mistakenly identified with Progress), the enshrined mode of thinking called cost-benefit analysis (mistakenly identified as the most valid methodology), strenuous attempts to operationalize all aspects of human existence (mistakenly called the 'rationalization' of life) are all part and parcel of the same philosophy.

We are training Bazarovs in our academic institutions. Indeed these institutions are set up to train and produce Bazarovs. The problem is severe, for even if we are dimly aware of the fact, we cannot help it: *Bazarovism, as an overall social philosophy, has pervaded the fabric of our society and the structure of academia.*

A most alarming aspect of the situation is that the Bazarovs still consider themselves 'the torch of progress', 'the vanguard of humanity', 'the remakers of the world for the benefit of all', while in fact they serve the most crass interests of the status quo, are in the vanguard of ecological and human devastation, and embody nothing but conformity and servitude. Within a mere hundred years 'revolutionaries' and 'progressivists' have become staunch defenders of the status quo. Such a dialectic of history may startle even well-seasoned dialecticians. Over the last decade the real revolutionaries, who have attempted to rekindle our interest in the wellbeing of humanity as a whole, have been not the toughminded rationalists, the ones who have been 'sweeping aside the rubble of history' to pave new ways, but the 'soft-minded' believers in intrinsic values, sometimes mystically inclined, often hostile to science and progress. As a result of these distressing shifts in the meaning of the terms 'reason', 'unreason', 'liberation', and 'oppression', liberals do not know what to believe in. They invested too much in Reason and Progress, which were meant to provide safeguards against oppression and exploitation, but in the meantime Reason has become a form of oppression and Progress a force of mutilation. Herbert Marcuse has convincingly made the case for this reversal in *One Dimensional Man* and his other writings, so we need not belabor the issue here.

The intellectual climate of the twentieth century – in the economically developed countries of the West, that is – has not only favored the rise and dominance of the Bazarovs. It has also contrived to inhibit everyone else from considering values as one of the central concerns of human thought and human life. One of the great misfortunes of modern Western thought has been the linking of intrinsic values with institutionalized religion. The bankruptcy of one form of institutionalized religion was tantamount, in the eyes of many, to the bankruptcy of religion as such, and of the intrinsic values woven into that religion. This identification was based on faulty logic. Religion, and especially intrinsic values, are not tools of the clergy to keep the masses in order (though occasionally they have been used for that); they are forms and structures, worked out over the millennia of human experience, through which the individual can transcend himself and thereby make the most of himself or herself as a human being, through which man's spirituality and humanity can acquire its shape and maintain its vitality, through which we define ourselves as self-transcending beings. As such, intrinsic values outline and define the scope of our humanity.

The climate of the twentieth century has anaesthetized us to our own spiritual heritage. Twentieth-century philosophy has done little to remedy the situation. Logical positivists have been notorious in manifesting their *insensitivity* to the problem of values. Even outstanding thinkers and well balanced philosophers, such as Sir Karl Popper, who has gained a reputation for being an anti-positivist, offer us precious little. Indeed, it is incredible (if not actually embarrassing) how little Popper has to say about values and how pale even that is. The shadow of positivism has engulfed us all. The value-vacuum has been an inevitable outcome of the attrition of religion and the emergence of a secular worldview.

3 *Information–Knowledge–Wisdom*

Copernicus is often singled out as a divide separating the Middle Ages from modern times. His views on knowledge, however, are closer to Plato and Augustine than to modern empiricists, for all three regarded knowledge not as a stock of facts and information held in the repository of memory but as an intrinsic part of being human. All three thought of knowledge as inseparable from a person's actions and judgements, so that correct knowledge, in the Augustinian sense, is the basis of proper conduct. Even Newton, though considered by empiricists to be their greatest asset, was far from thinking that knowledge was 'mere information', irrelevant to or independent from man's other concerns. Newton explicitly attempted to show the perfection of God through the harmony of his universe, which, he contended, revealed itself through the unity of the laws of physics governing the behavior of both terrestrial and celestial bodies.

Something happened between 1700 and 1900. We divided man into halves. We separated man's knowledge from his essence, from his values, from his transcendental concerns. Knowledge became isolated, put into a special container called brain. This container came to be regarded as a chest of tools: we pick up from this chest this or that tool for the task

at hand. There is no longer the unity of man and his knowledge. There are only specialized tools to handle specialized
tasks. At this point knowledge becomes mere information.
Soon it becomes translated into 'bits' of computerized information. The whole process is de-personalized, mechanized,
computerized.

The separation of facts from values, of man from his knowledge, of physical phenomena from all 'other' phenomena,
resulted in the atomization of the physical world, as well as
of the human world. The process of isolation, abstraction and
estrangement (of one phenomenon from other phenomena),
a precondition of the successful practice of modern natural
science, was in fact a process of *conceptual alienation*. This conceptual alienation became in turn human alienation: man
estranged himself from both his knowledge and his values.
The primary cause of contemporary alienation is a mistaken
conception of the universe in which everything is separated
and divided and in which the human being is likewise
atomized and 'torn'.

Our present compartmentalization is unnatural. In order
to restore our sanity and to recompose our divided selves we
have to rethink certain basic premises. To begin with, we
have to realize that *the state of one's knowledge is an important
characteristic of the state of one's being*. This is a re-statement of
the view of knowledge held by Plato, Augustine and Copernicus. This view is still held among primitive societies, notably among certain American-Indian tribes.

The statement that our knowledge is an important aspect
of our being, that as total bio-social organisms we cannot and
do not act independently of our knowledge, is not an expression of nostalgia for paradise lost. It is a statement describing
the human condition. How can we validate such a claim,
particularly at a time when knowledge seems to be quite
divorced from life? If the integration of relevant knowledge
is indispensable for the coherence of one's life, it necessarily

follows that to deprive people of such knowledge may be a source of confusion and incoherence in their lives. One does not have to be an astute observer to perceive that this is exactly what has happened in the contemporary period. Young people (and not only the young) are lost, confused and alienated because they do not have relevant knowledge to guide them; they do not have a compass, a sense of center that would make sense of the world around them. Instead they are furnished with bits of information and data, with expertise which they so often find to be irrelevant knowledge.

It is a pathological situation: knowledge does not provide enlightenment but confusion; the amassing of information only furthers the process of alienation. The situation is especially pathological because never in the history of mankind has learning (and supposedly knowledge) been pursued on such a vast scale as today, and never has the estrangement of man from the world, and from his fellow man, been greater than today. The cause must lie, then, in the nature of the knowledge we pursue. Knowledge alienated from the human mind and human values in turn de-sensitizes and alienates the people who acquire that knowledge.

But let us be very careful when we say that this knowledge is 'irrelevant'. For in one sense it is very relevant: it is relevant to the economic system, which is mainly interested in the maximization of profit. It is relevant to the technological society as we know it. It is relevant to the conception of the world as a factory. The system of economic, ecological and human exploitation is not interested in knowledge, let alone wisdom. But it is vitally interested in information and expertise; it is interested in its own smooth functioning, which is based on technological efficiency. For this reason we furnish our students and ourselves with information and expertise, not with knowledge.

Let us ask ourselves a very general question at this point. Is there one underlying reason for this eclipse of values and all the other ills that follow from it? Perhaps the most succinct answer to this question was given by Max Scheler, who said: 'To conceive the world as value-free is a task which men set themselves on account of a value: the vital value of mastery and power over things.' We realize nowadays that this mastery has been an illusion, that we cannot subdue the world to our will without destroying, or at least seriously impairing ourselves. Nevertheless we maintain and perpetuate the system which was designed for this grand, but ultimately pitiful, folly.

There is another general question which should be raised, namely, the question of the relation of theory to practice. The separation of values from knowledge may be seen as an abstract philosophical matter on one level. But this separation is an indispensable part of the process of turning people into Bazarovs, in order to maintain the present consumer society and the conception of the world as a factory. Let us not complain that there is no relation between theory and practice. There is: ingenious theories have been created and developed in order to justify and maintain parasitic practices with regard to other people and nature at large. It should be emphasized that the system parasitizes people and nature equally. It is of the greatest importance that we understand the relation between the economic forces of a society and its conception of nature and of the universe, between our daily practices and the view we hold of the world. These broader outlooks, or world views, imposed on us subtly and sometimes insidiously, justify and motivate our daily practices. And let us be clear that if we accept the scientific world view with its underlying rationality and its extension – modern technology – we have lost from the start. For this world view conduces to and justifies: turning knowledge into information, values into economic commodities, people into experts. The perilous aspect of modern science lies in the consequences it has led to, lies in the requirements and demands that it implicitly makes on people and the eco-system. It is useless to argue that it is not science that did the harm but the people who applied it. Knowledge is inseparable from people. Science has molded people's minds quite as much as people have molded science. The twilight of scientific reason, which we are witnessing today, is not necessarily the twilight of humanity. Scientific reason will have to wane and to release us from its overpowering tentacles so that we can repair the strained relation between knowledge and values.

Which brings us once more to the phenomenon of knowledge as an inherent aspect of one's being. This phenomenon manifests itself not only in frustrated and alienated youth, whose knowledge does not guide them because they are filled with irrelevant bits of information, but also in the converse phenomenon: our veneration of and craving for wise people. Wise people are the ones whose knowledge matters, are those who are in the state of being in which knowledge matters, are the integrated ones, in the sense that their knowledge serves them as human beings. We envy them because it is a state difficult to achieve in the contemporary world. Their wisdom is simply the integration of knowledge with values; it is a demonstration that knowledge is not a futile store of information but a vital force that sustains life at all levels of human existence; it is a resurrection of the universal property of knowledge, the unity of life and knowledge.

The re-integration of knowledge with values will have to take place not in order to make each of us a sage, but in order to assure the survival of humanity. It should be abundantly clear to us that we shall not be able to cope with the plethora of problems which the present (scientific-technological) mode of our interaction with nature and other people has originated, until we again arrive at a stage in which our knowledge matters to us as human beings. This will be a knowledge intertwined with values and at their service. This knowledge will be a re-embodiment, on a new level, of Plato's and

Augustine's contention that to think correctly is the condition of behaving well; with this proviso, however, that to think correctly is not merely an abstract characteristic of the brain but an expression of a state of being; a combination of intellectual insight and moral power.

This state of being, which is still maintained in wise people, is akin to the state of grace. The term 'grace' is extremely loaded. Every 'self-respecting intellectual' avoids it. But its past religious connotation should not deter us from making good use of it, for this term makes us clearly aware that to think well is not to think dexterously, ruthlessly, logically: to think well requires a special state of mind and of the entire being. This state of mind needs to be cultivated and nurtured as much as we cultivate – in long years of abstract thinking – the mind geared to 'scientific objectivity'.

We have a great deal to learn from oriental cultures, from the history of our own civilization, and from primitive societies alive today, in understanding, acquiring and maintaining this state of mind in which 'thinking well is a pre-condition of behaving well'. What is involved is not the acquisition of another piece of knowledge – of how 'other' societies thought and acted – which we shall append to our existing knowledge, but a change in the structure of our knowledge and in the structure of our mind which will lead, so we should like to hope, to the healing of the value-knowledge split and to the elimination of a great deal of our present alienation.

This fundamental change will resolve many specific problems which trouble us daily, such as: how can we know what research to pursue? How do we assess whether a piece of research is beneficial or detrimental? The answer to this question (in a simplified form) is: in order to pursue good research we have to pursue a good life; we have to think 'correctly' in the all-embracing meaning of the term 'correctly'. This kind of thinking is much more difficult than mere abstract, atomistic, analytical thinking. If it seems to some as if I were saying that one has to be in a state of grace in order to do good research, they are not far from the truth. For the present mutilation of the world around us, and of other people, is directly attributable to an attitude of mind which is *graceless*, which represents the disinherited mind, the subservient mind, and which is unworthy of creatures calling themselves human beings.

Should anyone seek to condemn this attitude, which we tentatively call 'grace', as a return to pre-scientific prejudices, obscurantism or the like, we would reply: why should a state of mind in which abstract entities called 'facts' are enshrined as deities be preferable to a state of mind in which intrinsic values are so enshrined? For our 'state of grace' is simply another expression for the state of mind in which intrinsic values are enshrined. When we say: 'Dignity is an essential component of being human'; 'Freedom is a necessary requirement of the concept of humanity', we in fact 'engrace' man. We have to change the world around us, and the frame of our minds, and the structure of our knowledge so that these expressions are not phrases empty of meaning.

To sum up, over the last three centuries we have redefined the world around ourselves and those redefinitions have resulted in a violation of the world about us and of ourselves. We have to discard a great deal of the 'wisdom' of the prophets of material progress, for this progress is leading us to doom. We need to remove many spurious dichotomies and distinctions, for they are often at the root of alienation in the present-day world. Above all, we have to restore the unity of knowledge and values; we have to realize that wisdom or 'enlightened knowledge' is the key to human *meaning*. We also have to develop a new comprehensive philosophy which will make a new sense of the world around us.

NOTES

1. Present analytical philosophy is an embodiment of the positivist ethos, which is based on the cult of technique and the avoidance of problems. Analytical philosophy is not a liberation of the mind (as its practitioners want to insist), but a confinement of the mind in the circus of technical virtuosity. The endless debates over, for example, 'sense' and 'reference' by 'leading philosophers' of the 'outstanding intellectual centres', such as Oxford and Cambridge, Harvard and Princeton, Berkeley and Ann Arbor, is a curious spectacle. The same positions, arguments and resolutions have been repeated over and over again during the past fifty years! With Frege and Russell, Lesniewski and Tarski, the creative aspects of the problem have been explored and exhausted. The last forty years of the debate therefore represents tedious scholasticism resolving itself in pedantic linguistic exercises. The trivialization of problems and of minds is the price we pay for spurious technical virtuosity.

2

Eco-Philosophy Versus Contemporary Philosophy

1 *The Debacle of Contemporary Philosophy*

PHILOSOPHY, like life, is a process of perpetual re-examination, for philosophy is a peculiar distillation of a conscious part of our life. It is an important part of our image of ourselves, which we form in interaction with the external world, with our past history, with our future dreams. Without philosophy, we have no anchor, no direction, no sense of the meaning of life. Each epoch and each society is rooted in some fundamental beliefs and assumptions, which are acted upon as if they were true. They justify all other things that follow from them, while they themselves are accepted on faith. A change in philosophy is a change in the accepted canons of faith, whether that faith is of a religious or a secular character. And conversely, when a given people, society or civilization is shaken or shattered, this calls for fresh thinking; in fact, more often than not, for a new philosophical basis.

It would be commonplace to repeat that our civilization has lost its faith, confidence and direction and needs a new philosophical basis to get out of its present swamp. It would be commonplace to repeat that past philosophies, including the twentieth-century analytically-oriented, Anglo-Saxon philosophy, came into being as the result of a specific distillation of the twentieth-century Western mind, and as such was not only justifiable but perhaps even inevitable. Again, it would be commonplace to observe that when society and civilization take a new turning, philosophy must re-examine its positions, shake off the dust of its dogmas and be prepared to be impregnated with new ideas and a new vitality. However, such a process of radical intellectual rethinking cannot be accomplished without some resistance and some pain; for we are all, even philosophers, partial to our dogmas and our mental habits.

Let it be remembered that ours is the age of specialization. And what do we expect of a specialist? That he knows one thing well – even if he is an ignoramus otherwise – that he is thoroughly drilled in this one single thing, and that he is proud of being a narrow technician. In a heaven where the ultimate god is a technician, all the smaller gods are technicians too.

In so far as present-day philosophers stand up to the challenge of the technical age and show their prowess as virtuoso technicians, they are admirable – for technical virtuosity meets with applause in a technical age. In so far as they have had to renounce a part of the great philosophical tradition and drastically narrow the scope and nature of their problems for the sake of the virtuosity, they disappoint.

But perhaps the philosophers are not to blame; not entirely at any rate. They are simply following the *zeitgeist*. The whole of civilization has gone topsyturvy in its zeal for specialization. We are a schizophrenic civilization which deludes itself that it is the greatest that has ever existed, while its people are walking embodiments of misery and anxiety. Our knowledge and philosophy only widen the rift between living and thinking. T. S. Eliot's prophetic cry: 'Where is the Life we have lost in living? Where is the wisdom we have lost in knowledge? Where is the knowledge we have lost in information?' rings today truer than ever. (From: 'Choruses From The Rock').

Philosophers thrive on challenges, for every new philosophy is a challenge *par excellence* thrown to the limits of our comprehension of the world. We are now in yet another period of ferment and turmoil, in which we have to challenge the limits of the analytical and empiricist comprehension of the world just as we must work out a new conceptual and philosophical framework in which a multitude of new social, ethical, ecological, epistemological and ontological problems can be accommodated. The need for a new philosophical framework is felt by nearly everybody. It would be lamentable if professional philosophers were among the last to recognize this. I sense that many of them are diligently groping towards new vistas. Philosophy is a great subject, it has a great past, and a great future. Its present lowly state is an aberration and an insult to its heritage.

Martin Heidegger once remarked that one just does not write books on metaphysics. Metaphysics, and in a sense all philosophy, is a response to the challenge of life, to the challenge of actual problems which are thrust upon us with irresistible force. Genuine metaphysics involves a significant rethinking of the problems of man and the world in any given time. In this sense Eco-philosophy seeks to provide a new metaphysics for our time. And in this sense the various treatises on metaphysics which analyze only the logical structure of propositions, or attempt to force various levels of being into prearranged semantic boxes, are chasing but a shadow of a fading world.

When Wittgenstein proposed his Logical Atomism it was a genuine metaphysics because it grew out of a real and nagging problem, which was to re-establish solid and coherent foundations for mathematics. It was thought absolutely vital that at least mathematics should be firmly anchored. It was hoped that mathematics, *via* logic, would provide secure foundations for all other branches of knowledge. Moreover, at the time, the new mathematical logic – which was ingeniously used later as the conceptual backbone of Logical Atomism – promised to put an end to the chaos of philosophy

and also to establish a system of scientific philosophy far
superior to anything that had ever existed. Therefore, given
the state of knowledge at the time, and given the aspirations
of an epoch which still believed in salvation through science,
logic, and technological progress, and actually wanted salvation in these terms (one must never discount the aspirations of
the epoch as well as the unwritten longings which prompt
thinkers and philosophers to move along specific paths),
Logical Atomism was a bold, ingenious, and justifiable ven-
ture. Furthermore, given the state of knowledge and the state
of minds in the 1920s, Carnap's *Der Logische Aufbau der Welt*
(The Logical Structure of the World, 1928), was still a legitimate metaphysical proposition, though tending to burst at
the seams because it attempted to stitch together too much,
too neatly. Perhaps Willard van Orman Quine was the last
metaphysician of the epoch – the epoch which sought the
resolution of our major problems through logical structures.
But today's state of knowledge and today's aspirations do not
even remotely resemble those of the 1920s and 1930s. Consequently anyone still trying to turn philosophy into a neat
logical system is chasing a ghost from the past.

Let us pay homage where homage is due. Analytical philosophy has done much to liberate us from the spell of language.
And Wittgenstein rightly deserves to be hailed as the man
who did more than most to liberate us from that spell. But let
us recognize that Wittgenstein's philosophy has its own limits,
that it is now over forty years since *Philosophical Investigations*
was conceived and written, and that since that time we have
come to understand that the book constitutes no final tableau
of philosophical problems. Indeed our perspective has
changed during the last ten to fifteen years. We have come to
recognize that *emergent* philosophical problems are *never*
linguistic or analytical in nature. They are part of newly
emerging life forms, and as such require adjustments in our
ontology and epistemology, in addition to a new conceptual

and linguistic apparatus. At present we are once more beginning to be steeped in the problems of the 'real world'. The revision of the entire Wittgensteinian and analytical tradition is in progress. Now, being conceptually tough and linguistically dexterous (for this is what analytical philosophy best equips us with), we could go on playing linguistic games, and indeed fend off anyone who sought to break our linguistic cocoon; but this would be of no use. For the fact is that by now most philosophers know deep down that a new era of philosophy is coming, that the world expects philosophers to turn their minds to the new philosophical problems of our day, that the linguistic-analytical idiom renders elegant results but is limited in its scope, that we have been bewitched by Wittgenstein. This is ironic because he warned us not to become bewitched by language itself nor any set of utterances by any particular philosopher.

At the end of his life, the biologist C. H. Waddington, while rethinking the dilemmas inherent in the present state of biological knowledge, which he found to be the dilemmas of the present state of knowledge at large, blamed philosophy and philosophers for setting us on a wrong trail. He claimed (as have others) that philosophy took a wrong turning at the beginning of the century. Instead of following Whitehead, and his holistic and organistic philosophy, it followed Russell, and his atomist, mathematical philosophy. Waddington's advice was: 'Back to Whitehead', which is commendable. However, his diagnosis of the past is fraught with difficulties. For it seems to me that given the entire thrust of the epoch, its belief in progress, exactitude, science, and above all given the conceptual power of the tools of mathematical logic (with its definiteness, crispness, elegance and finality), the search for solutions *via* logic was too irresistible to allow us to follow Whitehead at an earlier time.

But now it is all different. Logical Atomism, Logical Positivism, the dream of the scientific system of philosophy, and salvation *via* linguistic hygiene, are all but history. And the present-day world is one in which scientific knowledge is tottering, a world in which the concepts of nature and of ecology are in urgent need of redefinition because they have become major philosophical problems. This is a world with unprecedented social and individual afflictions, many of which, paradoxically, have been brought about by a seemingly benign technology which has become our crutch to the extent that we are unable to think and act on our own.

In outlining the scope of what I call Eco-philosophy, I shall be pleading for a new philosophy which actually marks a return to the great tradition of philosophy – the tradition that takes upon itself large tasks and attempts to be culturally significant. Since I wish to go beyond the canons and precepts of contemporary philosophy, I cannot be constrained by its criteria of validity. Eco-philosophy, here presented, is offered as a challenge. It possesses enough significant *problems* to make philosophers (and not only philosophers) reflect, ponder, re-examine, propose new insights and truths. Out of creative combats and lively encounters new truths are born; while reciting old truths, whether of Hegelian or analytical philosophy, will only produce a deepening dullness of mind. It is a mark of the enlightened mind to accept the terseness of the challenge with the equanimity of spirit and the generosity of heart characteristic of true searchers for new philosophical horizons. It is my wish that the tenets of Eco-philosophy will be received in this spirit.

Let me just add one terminological remark. When I say 'contemporary philosophy' I mean primarily current Western philosophy of the empiricist, analytical, scientific school, since this is the philosophy which not only dominates the Anglo-Saxon universities, but has, indirectly, become the accepted global philosophy. When the Arab countries talk about progress (or an Arab sheikh buys his Mercedes, for that matter), when people talk about the Green Revolution or about bringing education to the illiterate of the Third-World countries, it is all done within the implicit context of a Western empiricist, positivist, analytically-based philosophy. All major economic transactions in the world are an endorsement of our Western philosophy.

I am aware that there is a difference between Logical Atomism and Husserlian Phenomenology, between the philosophy of the later Wittenstein and Sartrean Existentialism – all Western products. But I am also aware that phenomenology and existentialism have little influence on and do little harm to the world or those private individuals who adhere to their tenets, while empirically oriented positivist philosophy, particularly as developed in the Anglo-Saxon countries, provides the philosophical justification for the ruthless, exploitative, mechanistic paradigm which has wreaked so much havoc on world ecology, on Third-World nations and on individuals who have attempted to mold their lives in the image of the machine. And it is this version of contemporary philosophy that Eco-philosophy stands against and to which it attempts to provide an alternative.

I am also aware that perhaps none of the present analytical philosophers will recognize himself in my reconstruction. I am not analyzing any particular philosopher, nor any set of philosophers, but the essence, and above all the consequences, of the whole philosophical mode of thought of an epoch. Most of all, I am investigating what changes must be made in this mode of thought to make philosophy a truly supportive tool in our quest for meaningful living.

It is precisely this simplistic, linear, atomistic, deterministic – in short, scientific – thinking, that chops everything into small bits and subsequently forces the variety of life into abstract pigeonholes of factual knowledge which I consider diseased, for in the final reckoning it produces diseased consequences. Therefore, when I say that in devising new tactics for living we shall need to rethink our relationships with the

world at large, I mean expressly that we shall need to
abandon the mechanistic conception of the world, and replace it with a much broader and richer one. Eco-philosophy
attempts to provide the rudiments of this alternative
conception.

What is Eco-philosophy? How does it differ from what we
have agreed to call contemporary philosophy? I distinguish
twelve characteristics, which I shall compare with the corre-
sponding characteristics of contemporary philosophy. To
heighten the contrast I shall start with two diagrams, both
of which will be explained in detail as we go along.

2   *The Characteristics of Eco-Philosophy*

(a) *Eco-philosophy is life-oriented*, as contrasted with contemporary philosophy which is language-oriented. Life is not
a 'terminal cancer', as some medical practitioners maintain,
but a positive phenomenon with a force and beauty of its
own. Those who cannot recognize life's positive vector have
already retired from it and allowed themselves to drift into
the abyss.

We do not have to justify our partiality to life, for what
is more important than taking life seriously? Indeed, the
burden of proof is on analytical philosophers. They have to
show that their philosophy is of any use to life. We do not
intend to be crass about it and ask for some vulgar pragmatic
justification of philosophy, or tell them: 'Show me how your
teaching affects my life, or I will fire you'. But some justification must be given in the long run. An obvious one is to
suggest that language-rooted philosophy enlarges the scope
of our knowledge of both language and the world, and thereby assures enlightenment and provides better tools for living.
This 'thereby', however, constitutes a big leap; it is really an
article of faith, not a logical conclusion. The whole justifica-

tion fails if and when we observe that by acting upon this allegedly superior knowledge provided by science and scientifically oriented philosophy, we arrive at major ecological, social and individual pathologies. The point is that in their aloofness, or shall we say in their insularity, academic philosophers so often do not even bother to provide any justification for their philosophy. Philosophy is in the university curriculum. And this is good enough for them. However, life has its own ways of avenging.

Philosophy is essentially public and social. Sooner or later, life, through society, or some impertinent individuals, will ask: 'What are you doing, and what is it for?' Sometimes this question is posed to philosophers gently and indirectly, sometimes rather bluntly, as happened at Rockefeller University in 1976, when four distinguished philosophers were fired. So we have no need to be apologetic about maintaining that we want philosophy which is life-enhancing, for all philosophy has only one justification, the enhancement of life. The fact that there is a mountain of self-serving analytical reflection in which so many philosophers are completely buried does not mean anything except that there is this mountain of analytical reflection. We shall not deny that a great deal of brilliance, ingenuity, and strenuous effort went into those analytical ventures, but this will not prevent us from suggesting that a great deal of it was energy misspent because philosophy has locked itself in a hermetic cul-de-sac.

(b) *Eco-philosophy signifies commitment to human values, to nature, to life itself*, whereas academic philosophy spells out a commitment to objectivity, to detachment, to facts. All forms of life are committed. Life, as an ontological phenomenon, does not recognize objectivity and detachment. Objectivity is a figment of man's mind; it does not exist in nature. It can be argued that objectivity is a mode of assessment. If so, it is not rooted in the firm physical reality out there, but is only a

Diagram I
MANDALA OF ECO-PHILOSOPHY

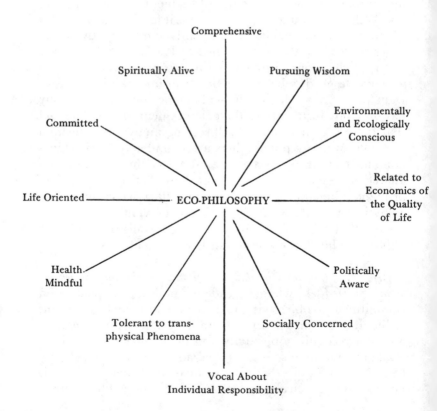

Comprehensive

Spiritually Alive

Pursuing Wisdom

Environmentally
and Ecologically
Conscious

Committed

Life Oriented — ECO-PHILOSOPHY — Related to
Economics of
the Quality
of Life

Health.
Mindful

Politically
Aware

Tolerant to trans-
physical Phenomena

Socially Concerned

Vocal About
Individual Responsibility

Diagram II
MANDALA OF PRESENT PHILOSOPHY

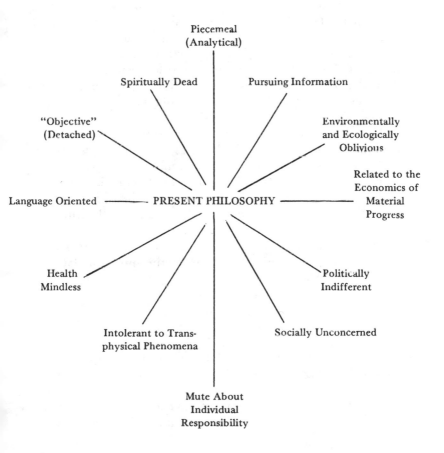

Piecemeal
(Analytical)

Spiritually Dead

Pursuing Information

"Objective"
(Detached)

Environmentally
and Ecologically
Oblivious

Related to the
Economics of
Material
Progress

Language Oriented ——— PRESENT PHILOSOPHY ———

Health
Mindless

Politically
Indifferent

Intolerant to Trans-
physical Phenomena

Socially Unconcerned

Mute About
Individual
Responsibility

disposition of the human mind. Let me repeat, objectivity is not an 'objective fact' residing out there. Has anybody seen it? Under a microscope, or through any other instrument? Now, if objectivity is to have its most solid justification in physics, then let us be aware that this justification is not solid at all, not only because of Heisenberg's uncertainty principle, but also because, in the last analysis, we have no way of validating what we grasp through our scientific theories: is it what is actually out there, or the behavior of the scientific instruments created in our own image? In other words, at some point of analysis, when we approach the problem of the existence of ultimate subatomic particles, the (objective) bottom falls out of atomic physics, and we seem to be close to Zen. We co-constitute existence through our perception; the observer is inseparable from the observed. (See Fritjof Capra, *The Tao of Physics*, 1975.)

The concept of objectivity is inseparably linked with the explosion of so-called methodologies, which are, in various disciplines, simply different ways of rendering the same myth of objectivity. The proliferation of methodologies is a menace. Although they were meant to be a tool, a help, in the long run they have become mental crutches, a substitute for thinking.

The fundamental questions 'How to live?', 'What is it all about?' are essentially different from the question 'How to do things?'. 'How to live?' belongs to the sphere of eschatology, which is concerned with ultimate goals. Methodologies, on the other hand, have a specific temporary terminus; they are concerned with specific changes in physical things, or specific ways of handling knowledge.

When eschatology is translated into, and short-changed for, methodology, the question 'How to live?' becomes the question 'How to do things?' This has been one of the tragedies of our times, namely that we have forgotten that there is no methodology which can give an answer to the question

'How to live?' Eco-philosophy maintains that it is a perversion of eschatology to translate it into a methodology.

It is a perversion of the meaning of human life to reduce it to consumption, limiting it to its physical, biological and economic aspects. Ultimate meaning and fulfilment are secured by those singular moments when our being reaches transphysical realms of aesthetic contemplation: of being in love, of deeper illumination when we grasp what it is all about, of religious and semi-religious experiences. All these are transcendental aspects of man's being, therefore transphysical and transobjective. We compassionately unite ourselves with the larger flow of life. No philosophy can succeed in the long run unless it attempts to understand nature and life in compassionate terms. Life is a phenomenon of commitment. In avoiding commitment, we are avoiding life. Philosophy that shuns life and a commitment to it is a part of the entropic process leading to death. The death wish of our civilization has pervaded its philosophical edifices. Eco-philosophy attempts to reverse the process.

(c) *Eco-philosophy is spiritually alive*, whereas most of contemporary philosophy is spiritually dead. I do not have to justify my quest for spirituality in physical terms. Your asking me would show that you understood nothing of spirituality. How could I even talk to you about spirituality? It would be as if I said: 'Admire the Aphrodite of Knidos,' and you asked me: 'What kind of marble is it made of, what are its properties, its chemical composition?' The Aphrodite of Knidos, as a cultural and spiritual phenomenon, begins where marble as a physical material ends. Similarly: 'Tomorrow, and tomorrow, and tomorrow,/Creeps in this petty pace from day to day/To the last syllable of recorded time' is clearly more than simply an expression of the poet's ignorance of the semantically correct use of language.

Spirituality is a subtle subject, difficult to define, and often difficult to defend. Many people reject it because of its traditional associations with institutionalized religion. Let me therefore hasten to reassure you that I am using the term in a newly emergent sense which has little to do with spiritualism, occult practices or established religious connotations. Spirituality, as I see it, is a state of mind – really a state of being. In this state of being we experience the world as if it were endowed with grace, for we ourselves are then endowed with grace. We experience the world as a mysterious, uplifting place. We experience the world in its transphysical or transcendental aspects. The first act of awe when man was struck with the beauty or wonder of nature was the first spiritual experience. Traditional religions certainly embody this form of experience, but by no means exhaust it. All great art, in its creation and in its reception, is a living expression of human spirituality. Reverence and compassion, love and adoration exemplify different forms of spirituality. The contemplation of great poetry is a spiritual experience *par excellence*.

In order to go beyond his merely biological universe, man had to refine the structure of his experience, his ability to respond to ever more subtle phenomena, his capacity to experience the world through his active intelligence and increasingly versatile sensitivity. Every act of perception and comprehension, when evolution has reached the cultural level, constitutes a subtle transformation of the world. Spirituality is making the physical transphysical. The world experienced spiritually is one in which the process of active transformation through the intelligence and through sensitivity is magnified.

Spirituality is, in short, an overall structure for generating our transphysical experience – almost an instrument, enabling man to refine himself further and further. Thus, on the one hand, spirituality is a state of being – a peculiar experience of human agents that makes them marvel at the glory of being human or makes them prostrate themselves with compassion or anguish toward other human beings. On the other hand, seen on the evolutionary scale, spirituality is an instrument of the perfectibility of man. In a sense, spirituality is synonymous with the quality of humanity.

It should be noted that the conception of spirituality I have outlined (although it is independent of traditional religions and treated as a natural phenomenon – an attribute of human existence) does not preclude the recognition of divinity. For in making himself into a transbiological being, man needed images and symbols in which his dreams and aspirations could be vested. These images and symbols were deified and institutionalized in various religions, and their presence helped man in his further spiritual journey. Looking at our cultural and spiritual heritage as a whole, we can say without a doubt that the existence of the sacred and the divine has been neither spurious nor incidental but quite essential to the making of man as a transcendental being.

Eco-philosophy is spiritually alive, for it addresses itself to the ultimate extensions of the phenomenon of man, and these extensions spell out the life of the spirit, without which we are not much more than the chimpanzees jumping from tree to tree. Much of present-day philosophy is spiritually dead, for it addresses itself to problems and realms which systematically exclude the life of the spirit. The language of that philosophy, its concept and its criteria of validity are such that, of necessity it must dismiss everything to do with spirituality as invalid or incoherent.

To inquire into the condition of man is to be led inexorably to the conclusion that man's essential quest is for meaning. This quest for meaning, whether through traditional cultures and religions, or through modern science, is a spiritual quest; it has to do with understanding what it is all about. Thus the essential nature of man is to try to grasp the stars, even if only to understand where his feet are. To pretend that those

ultimate matters are in the private domain of each individual
is to give the public domain to the greedy, the rapacious, the
exploitative. Great cultures and great civilizations were wiser
than that. Some philosophers would maintain that concern
with those spiritual matters, important though they are, is not
the business of *professional* philosophy. I would maintain that
they are mistaken. Philosophy does not have to occupy itself
with small and insignificant matters. It has an impressive record
in occupying itself with great and important ones. Eco-philosophy has the courage to return to those important matters.

(d) *Eco-philosophy is comprehensive and global,* while contemporary philosophy is piecemeal and analytical. Eco-philosophy is comprehensive not because it is uncritically confident
that it can grasp all and explain everything. Far from that.
It is comprehensive of necessity, as a result of the realization
that we have no choice but to look at the world in a comprehensive, connected and global way. Buckminster Fuller has
said that if nature wanted us to specialize, it would equip us
with a microscope in one eye and a telescope in the other.

The atomistic and analytical way is one in which almost of
necessity the trivial, the facile, the obvious and the physical
dominate. The ultimate texture of life requires an approach
which posits a variety of depths, which assumes that there are
things which defy easy analysis (analysis is, in a sense, always
easy for it assumes that things must fit the tools with which
we approach them) and which also acknowledges that these
are the things that ultimately matter. All eschatology is non-
analytical.

Eco-philosophy, perceived as global and comprehensive,
is a process philosophy which is integrative, hierarchical and
normative – self-actualizing with regard to the individual,
and symbiotic with regard to the cosmos.

One of the most delicate matters of knowledge and philosophy is that of truth. Eco-philosophy believes that truth is

a far more intricate affair than simply finding an adequate description for our facts within the frame of reference of physical science. We acknowledge that truth consists of a correspondence between reality and its description. The notion of reality cannot be simply exhausted by scientific frames of reference however.

As we all know, in ecology we assume a much broader frame of reference than in physics or chemistry. Consequently, a mere physical or chemical description of phenomena, when we are in the ecological frame, will not do. But ecology is not the ultimate frame of reference. Evolution provides a much broader frame, particularly when it includes the cultural evolution of man. So our concept of truth must be related to the frame of evolution at large – not to a static description of things within 'evolutionary theory', as provided by molecular biology, but within evolution unfolding, evolving, producing newly emergent forms. Ultimately it makes sense to relate the concept of truth to the *cosmic scale*, within which evolution occurs. However, there is a problem here: one has to be omniscient to grasp the place of particular phenomena in evolution occurring within the cosmic scale. Therefore, we must be exceedingly cautious when we handle truth, for so much depends on our adequately describing our concept of reality. Perhaps it would be closest to truth to say that all claims to it are approximations because there is only one truth about everything. Such a conclusion is not going to be comfortable to the mind which is used to rigid categorizations and to the ascription of truth to single statements. We know how constrained the physical frame of reality is, and how constrained are its 'truths.' The cosmic scale is harder to grasp and harder to live with. However, we should not be concerned with making things easy but with understanding their ultimate reality.

(e) *Eco-philosophy is concerned with wisdom* whereas most

existing philosophies are directed towards the acquisition of information. It is not easy to talk about wisdom without sounding pretentious. What is wisdom? Even the wise are at a loss to answer this question. Wisdom consists in the exercise of judgment, based on qualitative criteria, usually in conflicting situations. Judgment cannot be quantified, neither can compassion, which is often a part of judgment. Thus wisdom, too, is essentially unquantifiable; it is an embarrassment to the quantitative society as it defies its very ethos; but at the same time, paradoxically, it is a quality highly sought after as it is recognized that fact and measurement can carry us only so far.

Now, the influence of our present quantity-ridden society and our present quantity-ridden education – one is the mirror-image of the other – is so pervasive that we are positively discouraged from exercising judgment and are prompted to make decisions 'on the basis of facts'. 'Facts are not judgmental; facts do not judge', we are told. But there is a huge fallacy in this proposition, for in a subtle way facts do judge; facts are judgmental. To obey facts is to obey the theory and the world view which those facts serve and which they exemplify and articulate. Facts are thus imperious judgments on behalf of the emperor called the Physical Paradigm of Reality. There is no escape from judgments – even when we accept the judgment of facts.

Wisdom is the possession of *right* knowledge. Right knowledge must be based on a proper understanding of the structural hierarchies within which life cycles and human cycles are nested and nurtured. E. F. Schumacher writes: 'Wisdom demands a new orientation of science and technology towards the organic, the gentle, the non-violent, the elegant and beautiful.' Ultimately wisdom must be related to our understanding of the awesome and fragile fabric of life. For this reason alone it must entail compassion, for compassion, properly understood, is one of the attributes of our knowledge of the world. It is a crippled school in which compassion and judgment are not developed. It is a crippled society in which judgment and compassion are neglected, for they are essential to acquiring some rudiments of wisdom – without which life is like a vessel without a keel.

(f) *Eco-philosophy is environmentally and ecologically conscious,* whereas contemporary academic philosophy is very largely oblivious to environmental and ecological concerns. It is of course so by definition, though there is a great deal more to Eco-philosophy than simply caring about our natural resources. Being ecologically conscious not only means taking judicious stock of existing resources and advocating stringent measures to make them last longer; it also entails reverence for nature and a realization that we are an extension of nature and nature an extension of us. Human values must be seen as part of a larger spectrum in which nature participates and which nature co-defines.

It may be argued that it is unfair, and indeed far-fetched, to accuse contemporary philosophy of lack of concern with ecology when it is simply silent on the subject. This is precisely the point: by its silence it participates in the conspiracy of indifference. Crimes of silence are particularly reprehensible in those who ought to be aware. Besides, contemporary philosophy indirectly endorses the view that everything is a matter for specialists and that, therefore, questions concerning the environment and ecology are to be left to the specialists, to economists, politicians, engineers, managers. Any philosophy worthy of the name must perceive that our views on ecology and the environment are always pregnant with eschatological, philosophical and ethical consequences.

(g) *Eco-philosophy is aligned with the economics of the quality of life.* Academic philosophies in the West seem to be unrelated to *any* economics but are in fact aligned with the economics of material growth. They function within the framework which not only tacitly supports but in fact engenders the ideal of material growth.

Western academic philosophers are empiricists or at least deeply affected by empiricism. They adhere, by and large, to the secular world view, recognize in material progress a valid measure of progress (and perhaps the sole definition of progress), and therefore clearly, though indirectly, support the modus of the economics of growth. The simple fact is that empiricism provides a philosophical justification for the economics of material progress.

Empiricism, material progress, and the economics of growth are all intrinsic parts of secularism conceived as a world view. Empiricism explains the world as being made of empirical stuff, material progress postulates that human fulfilment has to do with material gratification, while the economics of growth is the vehicle which secures the goods desired by material progress. There is no justification for the economics of growth in itself; its *raison d'être* is that it fulfils the requirements of material progress. Thus empiricism is the root, material progress the trunk and branches, and the economics of growth the fruit of the tree of secularism.

Eco-philosophy believes that an economics which undermines the quality of life is in conflict with life itself. Hazel Henderson, E. J. Mishan, E. F. Schumacher and others have shown the fatuity and meaninglessness of an economics geared to material growth alone.

The forces that determine the future of society, and of the individuals living in it, cannot be a matter of indifference to the philosopher. For this reason an understanding of economics, in terms of its relationships with nature and in terms of its influence on present society, is certainly a philosophical undertaking.[1]

(h) *Eco-philosophy is politically aware*; it is also politically committed *but* not in a superficial way, however. Eco-philosophy is political in the Aristotelian sense: man is a political animal not because he craves power, but because his actions are pregnant with political consequences. In short, *we make political statements not so much by the way we vote as by the way we live.*

Take one specific and rather drastic example. The population of the United States produces over 360 million tons of garbage per year, which means 1.8 tons per year per person, or 10 pounds a day. No other country can even begin to approximate this feat. To shovel away this pile of garbage (which, according to one estimate, is enough to 'fill 5 million trailer trucks, which if placed end to end would stretch around the world twice'), American taxpayers contribute $3.7 billion a year towards garbage disposal. Compare this with some other annual spending figures: urban transport, $130 million; urban renewal, $1.5 billion a year.[2]

There is a clear political statement involved in this production of garbage. In participating in it one is participating in an orgy of waste, with all the consequences. One of those consequences is a peculiar kind of mental pollution: getting used to waste as a way of life. Now, in order that America can waste, other nations must contribute. And do they contribute on their terms? No, they contribute on America's terms. Why? Because in this technological world the suppliers provide their goods on the terms fixed by the consumers. And the result of it? Quite often gross injustices and inequities. The plight of the Bolivian peasant or the Brazilian plantation worker, indeed the plight of most Third-World manual workers, is directly linked to the way the industrial countries (the consumers) choose to conduct their affairs. The production of garbage is ultimately a political act through which we (indirectly) affect the lives of others. The equation, alas, is simple: the more garbage we produce the more adversely we affect other people who are at the supplying end. Looking

around, one can clearly see that political structures and
alliances are forged and maintained, sometimes with far-
reaching and not always pleasant consequences for local
populations, in such a way that oil and other natural resources can flow to the industrialized countries.[3]

(i) *Eco-philosophy is vitally concerned with the well-being of
society.* It regards society as an entity *sui generis* which possesses a life of its own. Consequently, society can neither be
reduced to individuals (or considered as a mere sum total
of particular individuals), nor can it be understood through
its 'outward behavior'. Society is the nexus and cradle of
aspirations and visions which are certainly transindividual.
Society is ultimately one of the modes of man's spiritual being.
Society is certainly many other things too: an instrument for
transacting business, an insensitive bureaucratic beast that
frustrates our quest for meaning. But ultimately it must be
viewed as an instrument of man's perfectibility; thus, in the
metaphysical sense, a mode of man's spiritual being.

The social contract by which we are bound is cooperative
by its very nature; it is only an acknowledgement of our belonging to the larger scheme of things called the cosmos. It is
quite clear that a compassionate, symbiotic and cooperative
conception of the cosmos, of necessity, implies a cooperative
conception of society, for society is one of the cells of the
cosmos in its evolution.

Academic philosophy includes as one of its components
social philosophy. But within its scope society is treated as if
it were an insect under the microscope: it is all analytical
scrutiny, with little concern for the well-being of society. It is
no accident that many contemporary philosophers regard
society as a mechanistic aggregate to be handled in terms of
observable behavior and by means of statistical laws. So we
are justified in saying that contemporary philosophy is unconcerned with society.

(j) *Eco-philosophy is vocal about individual responsibility.* It insists that in addition to the rights we crave, we are also bound by duties and obligations. The point has been made by Solzhenitsyn: 'The defence of individual rights has reached such extremes as to make society as a whole defenceless against certain individuals. It is time, in the West, to defend not so much human rights as human obligations.' But Eco-philosophy also observes that the sovereignty and autonomy of the individual must be restored so that he can exercise his rights and responsibilities meaningfully.

The world of the specialist is a world in which all sorts of crutches progressively supplant our limbs and other organs, including the mind; it is a world in which our will and imagination are slowly replaced by mechanical devices; our initiative by the central computer. There is no doubt that part of our crisis is a crisis of confidence, which is in direct proportion to our delegation of powers to the expert, the specialist, the machine. And a great deal of the violence in our society is the result of our frustrated quest for responsibility and initiative. Unable to do significant things on our own, we find an outlet for this frustrated quest in pathlological forms of behavior: violence, destruction, rape. (Rape is, on one level of analysis, an exercise of individual initiative, an upsurge of the individual numbed by the tranquillizers of the system.)

Eco-philosophy suggests and insists that *we* are responsible for everything, including the possibly fantastic transformation of the world to a degree approaching omega point, the end of time, at which man fulfils his destiny by becoming God (see Teilhard de Chardin, *The Phenomenon of Man*). Eco-philosophy is voluntaristic, but within the constraints of the natural order and a compassionate understanding of the cosmos. We are the new Prometheans who have the courage to light the fire of our imagination *de novo*; but we are also aware of hubris, and of the enormous responsibility that the carrying of the flaming torch entails.

(k) *Eco-philosophy is tolerant of transphysical phenomena.* The desire to understand the cosmos is as deeply rooted in man's nature as his impulse to survive in physical terms. Knowledge is therefore not only an instrument of survival, but above all the ladder which we climb to reach the heavens. We live all the time in a multitude of webs signifying different orders of being and spelling out the complexity of our relationships with the world. In this multitude, the physical web is just one. However, it is this particular web which has become the focus of our attention and the object of intense investigation. We have become so obsessed with it that we have nearly lost sight of all the other webs, although those other webs are always present. We know it. We are using a different sense of 'know', however, than the one that is officially acknowledged. We have great difficulty in expressing, in current language, this different sense of 'know', for current language has become monopolized, and in a sense perverted, by the physical web.

Eco-philosophy terminates this monopoly, as it calls for a pluralistic epistemology designed to investigate orders of being and orders of knowledge which are both physical and transphysical. To transcend physics and go beyond its universe is the kernel of all philosophy, for the term metaphysics stems precisely from the desire to go beyond physics. One of the basic preoccupations of philosophy through the millennia has been an attempt to penetrate orders of being beyond the physical.

Although our enterprise is ontological and cosmological, as we try to determine and map the heterogeneity of the universe and our relationships with it, our *problem*, at present, is epistemological. For there is a peculiar monopoly in epistemology which we have to break in order to be able to *talk* about other orders of being. If we do not do that, we shall be

rendered speechless by the proponents of the present epistemology, be they philosophers or scientists, who will invariably ask: how can you *justify* your claim, what is your
evidence for it? By 'justify' they mean physical justification,
in 'accepted terms', within the framework of accepted
empiricist epistcmology and its various tributaries called
methodologies. Thus 'justified claims' bring us back to the
one-dimensional empiricist universe. So, if we arc to arrive at
a pluralistic epistemology, we must go beyond this constraint.

Can you justify acupuncture? You simply cannot; that is,
if by justification you mean a satisfactory explanation of the
phenomenon in the currently acccpted empiricist frame of
reference. Also, how can you justify the reservoir of biological
knowledge which we all possess, on which we vitally depend,
and which we indirectly acknowledge when we refer to our
instinct, cunning, prescience, premonition, insight, wisdom,
compassion? Can you justify telepathy, clairvoyance, and
other paranormal phenomena? You cannot. But you cannot
dismiss these phenomena any longer with the exclamation
' 'tis all a quackery'. Philip Toynbee writes: 'One of the most
depressing aspects of the whole affair [the investigation of
paranormal phenomena] is that – at least during the last
seventy years of serious investigation – the scientific establishment has wallowed in rancorous and punitive obscurantism
which is truly reminiscent of the Inquisition.'

Eco-philosophy signals the beginning of a new epistemology: pluralistic, life-rooted, cosmos-oriented, in contradis-
tinction to the present one which is matter-rooted and
mechanism-oriented. One point must be firmly borne in
mind: a great deal of present philosophy, particularly the
analytically oriented, consists of mere footnotes to the empiricist epistemology. That epistemology, remember, indirectly represents a constraining universe conceived in the
image of a deterministic machine. So let us not get caught in

the toils of present epistemology and its various methodologies with their criteria of *justification, evidence* and *validity*, for
they are all a part of the cognitive Mafia, guarding the monopoly of the one-dimensional-objectivist-physical universe.
These methodologies are but ornaments engraved on a tomb;
they have nothing to do with life and with the epistemology of
life. Eco-philosophy insists that in the long run we must create
the epistemology of life. The task now is to clear the rubble
from the ground and expose the limitations of contemporary
philosophy in so far as it has become a deferential tool perpetuating a crippled and crippling conception of the universe.

(1) *Eco-philosophy is health-conscious*, whereas most schools of
contemporary philosophy ignore this question. We are physical aggregates in motion, but we are also luminous chan-
deliers emanating thoughts, emotions, compassion. Eco-
philosophy abolishes the Cartesian dualism of mind and
matter and regards the various states (or orders) of being as
parts of the same physico-mental-spiritual spectrum. The
whole story of the universe is of matter acquiring sensitivity
– to the point of awareness, to the point of consciousness, to
the point of self-consciousness, to the point of spirituality.
Reason itself is a form of sensitivity of matter. This whole
physico-mental-spiritual spectrum is our responsibility, and
maintaining our health is our responsibility. We are not
machines to be mended when one part is broken or worn out;
we are exquisitely complex fields of forces. Only when we
assume that man and the environment are made of fields of
interacting forces do we begin to understand what a fascinating story the maintenance of human health is, and how
miraculous it is when things are in order, and we are in a
state of positive health. To keep this field of forces in constant
equilibrium means being in touch with the variety of transphysical forces which contribute to that equilibrium. *To be in
a state of positive health is to be on good terms with the cosmos.*

New thinking about health is slipping through even to the heart of the establishment. Thus, John Knowles, President of the Rockefeller Foundation, writes in a 1978 issue of *Science*: 'Prevention of disease means forsaking the bad habits which many people enjoy . . . or, put another way, it means doing things which require special effort – exercising regularly, improving nutrition, etc. . . . . The idea of individual responsibility flies in the face of American history, which has seen a people steadfastly sanctifying individual freedom while progressively narrowing it through the development of the beneficent state . . . the idea of individual responsibility has given way to that of individual rights – or demands, to be guaranteed by government and delivered by public and private institutions. The cost of private excess is now a national, not an individual responsibility. This is justified as individual freedom – but one man's freedom in health is another man's shackle in taxes and insurance premiums. *I believe the idea of a "right" to health should be replaced by that of a moral obligation to preserve one's own health'* (my italics).

Now, why should this concern with one's health be elevated to a philosophical proposition, when every boy and girl in elementary school is told: 'Take care of your health'? Within Eco-philosophy, taking care of one's health means taking responsibility for the fragment of the universe which is closest to one, expressing a reverence towards life through oneself; it is part of new tactics for living.

An aspect of our responsibility for our total health, or perhaps even its precondition, is recognition of the sanctity of life. The sanctity of life is not something you can prove with the aid of science. The sanctity of life is an assumption about the nature of life, particularly as perceived, comprehended and experienced by human beings. Recognition of its sanctity appears to be a necessary prerequisite for the preservation of a life worth living. Now, if I experience life as being endowed with spirituality and sanctity, who are you to dismiss my experience with a few titbits of empirical data? It is no good arguing that 'science does not lend any support to the supposition of the sanctity of life', for, in a sense, science does nothing. It is people, enlightened or unenlightened, rapacious or compassionate, who use science to support their views, opinions and visions. But there is an issue here. Our perception and comprehension are carried out, made valid and meaningful, within a conceptual framework. The one based on science seems to preclude recognition of the sanctity of life. But this conceptual framework itself is a form of mythology. In insisting on the sanctity of life we are clearly operating in another conceptual framework.

All world views, like all civilizations, are ultimately rooted in mythologies. I am using the term 'mythology' not to signify a fable or a fiction but rather a set of assumptions and beliefs which form the basis of our comprehension of the world. The ancient Greeks had their colourful mythology. Medieval Europe had its religious mythology. All so-called primitive societies had their respective mythologies. For all its claims to the contrary, science is a form of mythology. It has its unwritten and unproven dogmas which are otherwise called the presuppositions on which science is based. It accepts uncritically and unapologetically a form of voodoo, otherwise known as scientific method. It worships certain deities, otherwise known as objective facts. It deifies certain modes of behavior, otherwise known as the pursuit of objectivity. It gives sanction to a certain moral order, otherwise known as neutrality.

As in classical mythologies, all these characteristics are interconnected and interdependent. Neutrality is a necessary moral ingredient to make the pursuit of objectivity a privileged, preferred, superior mode of behavior. Objectivity is, in turn, necessary for making 'objective facts' our deities. Making objective facts our deities in turn justifies scientific method, which is so conceived as to enable us to explore and enshrine precisely those kinds of facts. Objective facts and scientific method are, in turn, necessary to 'justify' the presuppositions of science, for those presuppositions are so conceived as to reveal to us only what scientific method allows for, in other words, what is contained in the notion of physical facts. The structure of the scientific mythology is no less complex than that of traditional mythologies, and no less self-defining.

I am neither deriding nor trying to diminish the importance of science. Mythologies are of major importance in the life of societies and civilizations. We cannot readily perceive that science is a form of mythology because science is the filter or telescope through which we interpret the world. When we use it, we perceive what it reveals; but very rarely what it is. Besides, tampering with science and its mythology means tampering with the whole reality science has constructed for us. We are reluctant to tamper with our basic view of 'reality' for this would create too great a challenge to our identity – which is partly formed by the scientific view of the world. We cling tenaciously to the mythology of science for so much of it was poured into us at school when we were of a tender, uncritical age. We cannot successfully challenge it, or liberate ourselves from it, unless we develop an alternative mythology. The creation of an alternative world view or an alternative mythology is the imperative of our times. Eco-philosophy offers itself as a possible candidate.

To sum up, let me emphasize that the first diagram is not a catalogue of the virtues of Eco-philosophy here proposed, but a graphic representation of the overall belief that until and unless we acquire a conceptual scheme (call it philosophy, if you will) which is comprehensive and encompassing enough, we shall not be able to accommodate and articulate the variety of new relationships which are necessary for an ecologically healthy and humanly harmonious world view.

Let us also notice the essential interconnectedness of the

two diagrams. Each signifies totally different paradigms. When we move around the individual components of each diagram, we notice that each component, in a subtle way, determines the next, and is itself subtly determined by the previous one. Contemporary philosophy cannot help being spiritually dead, for its universe is dead: inanimate matter, physical facts, objective logical relationships. For this reason, having at its disposal the concepts that are specific to this dead universe, it cannot help being socially unconcerned, for social concern is not an objective category. It cannot help being politically indifferent, for politics is too large for its scope. It cannot help being mute about individual responsibility, for the idea of responsibility is beyond its scope and jurisdiction. It cannot help pursuing information, for information consists in those bits that perfectly fit its requirements, while wisdom does not. It cannot help being environmentally and ecologically oblivious, for its hidden premise is that the environment is there to be mastered by man and exploited to his advantage. It cannot help supporting, if only indirectly, the pursuit of material progress. It cannot help being oblivious to health for, according to it, health is the province of the medical specialists. It cannot help being intolerant of, if not hostile to, transphysical phenomena, for they violate the universe of its discourse which it takes to be valid and immutable. Behind the crippling narrowness of academic philosophy looms the shadow of logical empiricism (with its conception of pseudo-problems) which was used as a hatchet to eliminate from the domain of philosophy the most significant and vital problems.

Now, if we start from a different cardinal premise, for example that philosophy is life-oriented and that its mission is the enhancement of life, then all the other characteristics of diagram 1, i.e. of Eco-philosophy, follow. The new philosophy must be spiritually alive in order to understand the human being, a spiritual agent. It must concern itself with wisdom, for man does not live by physical facts alone. It must be ecologically concerned and support the economics of the quality of life. Let me underscore some of the main conclusions of Eco-philosophy rather than reiterate its characteristics: Objectivity does not exist in nature. Wisdom is essentially unquantifiable. Life not based on qualitative criteria is meaningless. We make political statements not so much by the way we vote but by the way we live. Society is one of the modes of man's spiritual being. Pluralistic epistemology is tolerant of transphysical phenomena and embraces a variety of modes of being.

In his book, *A Guide for the Perplexed*, E. F. Schumacher maintained that one of the most urgent tasks of our times is a metaphysical reconstruction. Once we know what we are doing and *why*, other forms of reconstruction, including the economic one, will follow more swiftly. For it is undeniably the case that if our foundations are cracking, no partial reconstruction or repair at the top of our edifice will be of any avail. A number of writers, notably Hazel Henderson in her book *Creating Alternative Futures* (1978) and James Robertson in his book *A Sane Alternative* (1978), have explicitly endorsed Schumacher's programme and attempted to provide some parts of this reconstruction. But while their works have a more practical and economic orientation, I address myself to the very foundations, to the philosophical and value problems which lie at the core of our intended metaphysical reconstruction.

This, then, is the essential message of Eco-philosophy: we can affect every element of our social, individual, spiritual, ecological and political life, not separately, but by affecting them all at once. Moreover, unless we affect them all, none will be affected. This is at least a partial explanation of why so many excellent alternative schemes (like the Ecology Movement) seem to me to have failed. Their vision was too limited. They addressed themselves only to a part of our mandala and regarded that part as the whole.

Eco-philosophy is another chapter in our continuous dialogue with the ever-changing universe. In changing ourselves and our relationships with it, we are changing and co-creating the universe. Out of the lethargic trance of technological inertia, we are emerging with a heightened awareness of our destiny, which is to build a responsible world by assuming our own responsibility, which is to infuse the world with meaning and compassion, which is to carry on the unfinished Promethean story: the story of man unfolding – of which great systems of past philosophy are such a luminous and inspiring example.

NOTES

1. For further discussion of this point see Henryk Skolimowski: 'Rationality, Economics and Culture', *The Ecologist*, June 1980
2. See: Katie Kelly, *Garbage* 1973, p. 41
3. See especially, Ivan Illich, *Energy and Equity*, 1974

3

Ecological Humanism

I *At the Next Watershed*

TRADITIONAL humanism has emphasized the nobility of man, the independence of man, indeed, the greatness of man, who is cast in the Protean mould. This conception of man went hand-in-hand with the idea of appropriating nature to the ends and needs of man. Ecological Humanism is based on the reverse premise. It sees man as simply a part of a larger scheme of things: of nature and the cosmos. We have to transcend and abolish the idea of the Protean (and Faustian) man. The consequences of this reversal are far-reaching.

Ecological Humanism is not just another fancy label for the view that we should be less wasteful of nature; it implies a fundamental re-orientation of perception. In the past ecology and humanism have trodden their respective roads and belonged to different ideologies. Ecology, as a movement, has predominantly focused on the *devastated environment*. It has striven for alternative solutions and remedies in order to restore wholesomeness to the environment. Humanism, on the other hand, has mainly focused on the *devastated human being*. It has striven for solutions and remedies (to injustices and alienation, through the reform of social and political institutions) in order to restore wholesomeness to the individual.

In their partial visions neither humanism nor ecology has sufficiently grasped that the plight of the environment and the plight of man both have the same cause, the ill effects of which are equally visible in the Capitalist and Communist worlds.[1]

Since Socrates the philosophy of nature and the philosophy of man have developed along different, and sometimes antithetical routes. Ecology is a recent restatement of the philosophy of nature, while humanism (whatever its denomination), is an expression of the philosophy of man. This Western dichotomy between the philosophy of nature and the philosophy of man has been at the root of our mistaken notion that nature is 'there' to be harnessed, subdued and exploited.

Ecological Humanism marks the return of the unitary view in which the philosophy of man and the philosophy of nature are aspects of each other. The conjunction of ecology and humanism is not arbitrary but the fruit of a perception of the essential unity of the natural and the human world. Ecological Humanism requires a broadening of the concept of ecology to encompass the balance of the human environment; the natural world then becomes vested with the same 'value' as the human world. On the other hand, the ecological balance becomes a part of the human balance. As a result, the concepts of 'ecology' and 'humanism' simply merge into each other. Both ecology and humanism are a part of our enlarged vision of the evolving cosmos.

Ecological Humanism offers an authentic alternative to industrial society. It holds that:

(1) *The coming age is to be seen as the age of stewardship:* we are here not to govern and exploit, but to maintain and creatively transform, and to carry on the torch of evolution.

(2) *The world is to be conceived of as a sanctuary:* we belong to certain habitats, which are the source of our culture and our spiritual sustenance. These habitats are the places in which we, like birds, temporarily reside; they are sanctuaries in which people, like rare birds, need to be taken

care of. They are sanctuaries also in the religious sense: places in which we are awed by the world; but we are also the priests of the sanctuary: we must maintain its sanctity and increase its spirituality.

(3) *Knowledge is to be conceived of as an intermediary between us and the creative forces of evolution,* not as a set of ruthless tools for atomizing nature and the cosmos but as ever more subtle devices for helping us to maintain our spiritual and physical equilibrium and enabling us to attune ourselves to further creative transformations of evolution and of ourselves.

2   *Ethics and Cosmology Co-Define Each Other*

In the scientific world view, ethics and cosmology (the view of the universe) are completely separate from and have nothing to do with each other. This is particularly stressed by various schools of positivist philosophy; and it is clearly seen in the attitude called 'scientific neutrality'. But this is not how things are seen in pre-scientific world views; here the ethics of a people and their view of the physical universe co-define each other. In those world views which survived the test of time and were found sustaining by the people that adopted them, there is a *coherence* between the value system or ethical code of the people and their other beliefs, so that the universe appears to be a harmonious place, supportive of human strivings. That coherence is gone from the scientific world view. Already John Donne cried: ' 'Tis all in pieces, all coherence gone.' If we find the universe a hostile and lonely place it is our culture that has made it so for us. More precisely, it is our overall view of the structure and content of the universe – how things are, which are important and which are not, which beliefs are 'justified' and which are not – the philosophical presuppositions that mold our culture, which in turn molds the individual to respond positively to the cosmology by which the culture is originated and programmed:

cosmology → culture → individual

There is a feedback relationship between cosmology, culture and the individual human being. Within the scientific world view the individual finds himself estranged from the universe and indifferent if not hostile to nature, precisely because the scientific cosmology has made the universe a coldly inimical place for man.

Eco-philosophy attempts to bring back the coherence between man's value system and his view of the universe in order that each shall be an aspect of the other, as it is in traditional cultures. Eco-philosophy seeks to rescue the individual not with a superficial massage after which our ego is pacified while the rest of our being is still torn asunder but by means of a thoroughgoing reconstruction of our cosmology, which, with culture, constitutes the matrix of our well-being (or ill-being).

New forms of life are created out of the materials of old forms. New forms of culture must be built out of the spiritual heritage that has been handed down. Instant culture is phoney culture; instant spirituality is bogus spirituality. Consequently the ecological cosmology developed here and the new (ecological) imperative put forward here are derived from our past ethical and philosophical heritage. There is much in our past worth saving – much, indeed, that is superior to more recent acquisitions of ours. It is not, however, a resurrection of the old that is intended here but a fresh construction from materials in our moral and spiritual treasury.

The cosmology of the Bible may be deemed antiquated today but it did provide the individual with a remarkable feeling of security and a great sense of belonging. In the Bible the *universe* is seen as God's personal creation, constantly supervised by God. It is a purposeful universe, which serves the causes of God. We know some of the purposes and designs of God; to that extent the universe is knowable. We do not know some other designs and purposes; to that extent the universe is mysterious and unknowable.

Man is conceived of as the chosen creature of God. He is of enormous significance as the protégé of God, for he was created 'in the image of God'. But all other creatures are equally created by God. Man has dominion over them but not the right to exploit and destroy them (as some scholars, such as Lynn White, would wish to maintain).

Values regulate the relationships between God, the Creator, and Man, his creature. These are the values of personal relationships: between Man and God: spelling out the obligations of Man to God; and of man to man: spelling out the obligations of man to other men. Man lives in a small and rather harsh universe, and God is full of wrath. So those values are mainly harsh prohibitions. We should clearly realize that in this cosmology, values are binding *personal* relationships: of man to God, and of man to man, they do not connect Man with the Cosmos, or with Nature or even with other living things.

Now let us look at the structure and consequences of the scientific cosmology. Here the *universe* is conceived of as an infinitely vast *physical* system, working according to physical laws. It has no purpose; it has no causes; it serves no cause. The universe is knowable. It is apprehensible by means of factual knowledge. And this is the only *genuine* knowledge. From which it follows that whatever is beyond this knowledge is either unknowable or (in a certain sense) non-existent. It is a curiously empty universe, really an empty space with some galaxies thrown in here and there, in which man is an accident rather than a consequence of anything.

Man is here conceived of as an insignificant piece of furniture in the infinitely vast physical universe. He is but a lump of physical matter, an infinitesimal speck wandering through the immensity of physical space-time. Ultimately, according to some (La Mettrie, Skinner), he is a machine and subject to deterministic laws; according to others (traditional humanists), he is the terminal point of himself, the point of departure and the point of arrival. But even here he has no justification or significance beyond himself.

Values are man-rooted and there is no transcendence beyond man himself. When our knowledge assures us that there is nothing in the universe but physical matter and physical laws, and nothing to our destiny but to perish and be disintegrated into atoms, our only anchor seems to be our transient existence. The rise of individualism in our culture is an acknowledgment of the meaninglessness of everything beyond and above the individual. The ancient Greeks were much more individualistic than we have ever been, but they did not *need* a doctrine of individualism. Individualism in our culture, particularly in the Anglo-Saxon culture, has become a desperate search for substitutes for our lost center. The excesses of individualism are an expression of the paranoia of an uprooted culture and people, of man reduced to man himself, or to physical matter. The individual, within the framework of Western individualism, is a savage god who is a law unto himself. There can be no genuine and sustaining ethic built on such a foundation.

The other strain of our secularized ethic is that of instrumentalism. When the universe is conceived of as a clock-like mechanism of a huge factory, the only things that matter seem to be physical objects, physical processes and physical transformations. Progress becomes simply material progress, and the aspirations and achievements of people tend to be thought of more and more in quantitative terms. Goods-oriented aspirations and values require quantitative assessment. Materialistic beatitude is geared to the quantitative scale. In the absence of any accepted set of intrinsic values, instrumental values tend to become more and more universal, and equated with the ultimate criterion of all values.

There is, then, a clear relationship between our picture of the world – seen as a huge factory, within the confines of which physical knowledge enables us to understand and manipulate its workings – and our growing attachment to instrumental values, through which we manipulate the world, other people *and* ourselves. The instrumental imperative eventually gives rise to the technological imperative, which demands that man should behave according to the modes dictated by technology's drive towards increasing efficiency. The technological imperative, to which we are increasingly subjected in highly developed industrial societies, is a remarkable triumph of the mechanistic, deterministic and objectivist *modus operandi* in the realm of human affairs. The brute *modus* of the inanimate physical world is now grafted onto the delicate tissue of human life.

The secularization of the world and the instrumentalization of values did not happen overnight. But once the process started to unfold and to accelerate, the results came with a swiftness and decisiveness that brought about a mechanization of the world unprecedented in history. It is curious, if not astonishing, that this process, although copiously written about, is so little understood. We still consider values as detached from our world view, as a kind of private domain, almost independent of the vicissitudes of society and civilization. Witness those endless, insipid, impotent discussions about values, in which pretentious and sentimental claims are made to the effect that, if only we changed our hearts a little and became more charitable to each other, all would be well.

Such discussions are bound to be impotent if they do not realize that our hearts and hence our indifference to each other necessarily reflect the ethos of civilization and of the society which has conditioned us. They provide eloquent proof of the fact that there is little understanding that values are intimately connected with cosmology – that they mirror it, shadow it, justify it. Now, it has been a part of the heritage of positivism, that ruling philosophy of our times, to separate values from cognitive knowledge, and thus from knowledge about the world, and thus from the world itself. If positivism is taken to be the most explicit part of the overall umbrella that stands for the scientific world view, then this scientific view, as seen through the strategies and cognitive gambits of positivism, is vitally interested in keeping us confused about the relation of values to cosmology. Indeed, the scientific world view is interested in producing Bazarovs, as I argued in Chapter 2.

3   *Three Alternatives: Kant, Marx, Schweitzer*

That all was not perfect in 'the best of all possible worlds' (i.e. Western civilization) was seen as early as the seventeenth century, notably by Pascal. Many alternatives have been formulated since. Let me touch on three of these, because they are important for the construction of our ecological cosmology.

Immanuel Kant is of particular importance here, representing as he does a pivotal point in the development of the scientific world view, and also because he provided some answers to the dilemmas of human morality in the age of unfolding science which are of lasting value. Kant accepted the finality of physical laws. He thought, with others of that time, that physics revealed the ultimate laws governing the behavior of the physical world. He tried to solve two dilemmas at once. The first was: How is it possible that in spite of the notorious unreliability of our senses the physical laws which are based on sense data are final and irrevocable? He concluded that knowledge of physical laws is not arrived at via the mechanism of the senses, but via something that *makes* it imperative that this knowledge is both intersubjective and irrevocable. This 'something' is the structure of the mind with its fixed categories, which the physical laws only reflect.

Karl Popper is right in saying that science has given rise to all the important epistemological and ontological problems of modern philosophy. But Popper's frame of reference, indeed his universe is too narrow to enable him to notice Kant's second dilemma. In his discussion of Kant, Popper has little to say about Kant's attempt to solve this dilemma: If physical science provides ultimate knowledge and seems to embrace the whole universe, what is the place of man in this universe? Kant had too astute a mind not to realize that, if we grant to physical science the claim of its universality *over everthing there is*, then man dwindles to utter insignificance. Kant's solution was: 'The starry heavens above you and the moral law within you.'

This was a separation of the physical universe from the moral universe. It was also a declaration of the complete sovereignty of man, that is, vis-à-vis the alleged universality of physical laws. Hence Kant's moral imperative: we must treat every human being as an end in itself. *Act in such a way that you always treat humanity, whether in your own person or in the person of any other, never simply as a means, but always at the same time as an end.*[2] It was a far-reaching and bold response to all attempts to instrumentalize humanity, i.e. to turn the human being into a means to other ends.

There is a transcendental element in Kant's conception of man. Although separated from religion, man is regarded as, in a sense, sacred. The reverence with which he speaks of man as an end in himself makes us aware that man is a creature beyond clay and even beyond the stars. This conception of man, upheld by Kant and others after him, lingers on in our own conscious and subconscious awareness and has been a buffer zone against the growing encroachment of instrumental values.

Now, what about the relationship between Kant's ethical conceptions and his cosmological conceptions? It is Kant's transcendental idealism that binds the two together. The nature of human values is transcendental, and so is the nature of the physical world. Physics explores only the surface, the phenomena, the 'real' things, 'things in themselves'; the noumena are beyond the grasp of physics, beyond our understanding. Whether Kant created his transcendental cosmology in order to justify the transcendental nature of man is an open question. But there is no doubt that he was aware that a completely physical universe, which is completely knowable and describable in terms of physical laws, leaves little comfort and little meaning to man.

We may also wonder whether Kant's moral imperative, much admired on the intellectual level at least, has been ineffective in the social and human realm because it attempted to situate us in one world (transcendental reality) while society and civilization have consistently attempted to situate us in another empirical/pragmatic reality. To avoid schizophrenia (the natural consequence of being constantly torn by different conceptions of life), we gradually opted for empirical/pragmatic reality.

Kant's solutions to the epistemological dilemma, 'How can we acquire knowledge which is irrevocably certain through our notoriously unreliable senses?' and of the moral dilemma, 'How can we guarantee the sovereignty of man in a world governed by deterministic physical laws?' were both dazzling in their scope. But the relentless force which drove him was the conviction that the laws of classical mechanics were beyond refutation, and that they uniquely isomorphize physical reality (at least that part of it which is accessible to our comprehension). We no longer hold such a conviction for we consider *all* knowledge to be revocable and tentative.[3] Had Kant possessed our insight, or our hindsight, we would no doubt have thought up different solutions to both problems. His case is illuminating for two reasons. One is that great minds may conceive of marvellous solutions, even in the most constraining of circumstances (and the growing universality and rigidity of the physical structure of the universe was such a constraint). And quite another reason is that even the greatest minds are at the mercy of the assumptions of their times. All things considered, Kant's insistence on treating man as an end in himself is a salutary defence of the sovereignty of man against the deterministic universe.

Another alternative was that of Karl Marx. Though far more influential than Kant's, the Marxist alternative to the capitalist world view, when examined at all closely, turns out to be lamentably shallow and inadequate.

In the second half of the nineteenth century and the first half of the twentieth century, Marxism was seen by many as the only worthy alternative to the capitalist system. Yet Marxism shares the fundamental assumptions of the post-Renaissance civilization which produced science, modern technology and modern capitalism. Marx was a complex and profound thinker. We do not really know which was dearer to Marx's heart: the liberation of man qua *being* or the perpetuation of the Enlightenment qua *science*, for Marx was enormously impressed and influenced by the ideas of the Enlightenment. We do, however, know one thing for certain – that, taken as a whole, marxism is a variation on the theme of secular salvation: the salvation of man through material progress, science and technology.

The Marxist cosmology is *aggressively* materialistic and carries even further the process of emptying the physical, social and human universe of spiritual and 'idealist' elements than the various traditional empiricisms. The label 'vulgar materialism' has therefore often been quite appropriate for

Marxist philosophy. But even when it is not limited to its extreme form of 'vulgar materialism', the Marxist cosmology represents a woefully restricted universe. Moreover, that universe (as rendered by Dialectical Materialism and Historical Materialism) is always nervously guarded against the possibility of infection by idealism – too quickly dismissed as 'religiosity' or a 'remnant of the bourgeois ethos'. When every scrap of energy goes into defending a cosmology against possible infections, there is little scope for positive living under its inspiration.

It has been a major tragedy for Marxism that it has had to fight on two fronts simultaneously: against existing society and against all religion. For in fighting against religion, it has cut itself off from the spiritual heritage of mankind even more profoundly than the 'bourgeois philistine ethos' itself. Had Marxism embarked on both social and spiritual renovation, the history of this century might have run a different course. But perhaps this was not possible. The arrow of time was pointing in a different direction. 'Progressive' movements had to become even more secular, even more steeped in the anti-religious 'Enlightenment', so that the drama of the secular civilization could unfold to its final act. *The Marxist ethic has proved both unsustaining and crippling, for it was built on the same inadequate world view as our own.*

Albert Schweitzer's alternative lacked the scope of either Kant or Marx, but he was perspicatious enough to realize that the basic problem was one of values. As he saw it, 'The ideals of true civilization had become powerless, because the idealistic attitude toward life in which they are rooted had gradually been lost to us.' He was also acutely aware that it was not enough to criticize civilization and its ills; one had to try to build something constructive. His constructive contribution was an ethics based on *reverence for life*. As he wrote of the moment when, after many struggles, his new ethical principle finally dawned on him: 'Now I had found my way to the idea in which affirmation of the world and ethics are contained side by side!' (From: *My Life and Thought*, London 1948, p. 185.)

Schweitzer's ethic of reverence for life is a remarkable anticipation of the ecological ethic; we should say, perhaps: the ecological ethic-in-the-making. Yet, there is a subtle problem here. The principle of reverence for life is known and on occasion spoken of, but the content of it is only superficially absorbed. Listening carefully to the arguments and reasons for the ecological ethic, we so often find that the reason why we should take care of the ecological habitat is because it takes care of us. It would be counterproductive to destroy it, therefore we should preserve it. It is a principle of *good management* to take good care of our resources. So, in the final analysis, the ecological habitat becomes a *resource*. The ecological ethic is thus based on a calculus of optimization of our resources. It becomes an *instrumental* ethic: the ecological habitat is not a value in itself but only an instrument, a means of supporting us.

It is at this level of analysis that a fundamental difference appears between Schweitzer's principle of Reverence for Life, which proclaims the intrinsic and sacred value of life itself – 'A man is ethical only when life, as such, is sacred to him' – and the seeming worship of the ecological niche, which is but a worship of our physical resources. Now, is there an irredeemable incompatibility between the two? Might it not happen that the ecology movement adopted Schweitzer's principle, particularly as some people are half-consciously groping in this direction? It might indeed. But if it is to happen, many ecology-minded people will have to discard the technocratic and instrumentalist mode of thought.

There is another reason why Schweitzer's teaching has had less influence than it deserves. He was a Protestant pastor to begin with, and never ceased to be one. The institutionalized Christian religion was perhaps more precious to his

heart than his love of Humanity. He considered the value of
the Christian ethic to be universal, lasting and permanent,
and did not see any conflict between the principle of Reverence for Life and the Christian ethic. The point of fundamental importance is this: he did not see that it was the other
way around, that the principle of Reverence of Life and its
consequences spell out a much more general ethic, of which
the Christian ethic is a *particular* manifestation. Starting from
Reverence for Life, the Christian ethic follows as a consequence, but the converse is not the case; the pronouncement
of all life as sacred does not follow from the Christian ethic.
Of the former, Schweitzer was sometimes aware: 'The ethic
of the relation of man to man is not something apart by itself:
it is only a particular relation which results from the universal
one.' But he was too much a Christian to recognize the latter,
namely that the ethic of Reverence for Life *supersedes* the
Christian one.

There is a salutary lesson to be learned from Schweitzer.
To preserve man's sanctity and integrity, indeed to preserve
man as a human being, we must go beyond man himself.
There is no basis for the sanctity of man if man alone is his
own ultimate reference.

4   *The Promethean Heritage*

The relentless and heedless pursuit of material progress gives
birth, in time, almost with the inevitability of sinister hap-
penings in Greek tragedy, to the instrumental imperative and
the technological imperative, both of which become the
dominant moral imperatives of the technological society,
with the devastating consequences that this entails. Yet we
have to recognize that the pursuit of Progress is not an aberration of the human condition, but an expression of it. When
the ideal of Progress is radically impoverished, however, it

then becomes trivial progress and, ultimately, destructive progress.

The Promethean heritage is a part of our *moral* heritage. To be a moral agent is to be able to transcend the limitations of physical and biological determinants. To maintain a moral universe is constantly to engage in acts of transcendence. Progress in the real sense signifies the process of perpetual transcendence. The Promethean imperative stands for the necessity of transcendence. The Promethean imperative signifies Progress in the real sense.

The Darwinian notion of evolution and the consequences following from it are not a proof against the divinity of man; they do not 'conclusively reduce' man to the 'lower brutes' and ultimately, to unconscious and purposeless matter. On the contrary, looked at perceptively, even Darwinian evolution can be seen as a process of perpetual and increasing transcendence.

We have great difficulty in thinking of evolution as a benign process, for we have been conditioned to regard evolution within the framework of the competitive free enterprise system, in which evolution is construed as an expression of social Darwinism, and from which we are apparently to derive a moral lesson: either/or; either you suppress others, or others suppress you. Thus the notion of evolution is used as an ideological weapon: to justify and increase competitiveness and exploitation. The universe within this ideology is nothing more than an open market regulated by the entrepreneurial skills of those who are on top. Actually the universe itself may be thought of as an entrepreneur, but of a more subtle variety than the entrepreneurs of the Free Enterprise System.

At one time it was important to emphasize our links with the rest of the animal kingdom. This is no longer the case. As Theodosius Dobzhansky argues: 'From Darwin's time until perhaps a quarter of a century ago, it was necessary to prove that mankind is like other biological species. This task has been successfully accomplished. Now a different, and in a sense antipodal, problem has moved to the fore. This is to establish the evolutionary uniqueness of man. In several ways, mankind is a singular, quite extraordinary product of the evolutionary process. Biological evolution has transcended itself in giving rise to man, as organic evolution did in giving rise to life.'[4]

Evolution is a Promethean process, with hubris overwhelmingly present. At every juncture of this process, significant 'existential decisions' of great moral consequence were made. The transition from the amoeba to the fish was a great *moral* leap forward, for it enabled living matter to organize itself more satisfactorily on its way to explicit morality. The transition from the fish to the dexterous monkey was another moral leap forward. The transition from the principle, 'an eye for an eye' to the principle, 'Love thy neighbor and thine enemy', was an even greater leap forward. However, the announcement of the idea 'homo homini lupus' (Hobbes) was a moral leap backward. So it is no coincidence at all that the secular post-Renaissance ideology gave birth to empiricism and capitalism and to principles justifying cut-throat competition and extolling the concept of man as a 'wolf to man' and ultimately an enemy of life itself. The fact is that the *modus operandi* of our world view, as expressed through the working of its institutions, is undermining the biological versatility of life.

We have to look at the whole thing from an evolutionary point of view, from a perspective much larger than the confines of the technological civilization. If we accept the context and framework of the technological society, then the behavior of man according to the principle 'homo homini lupus' is not only justifiable, but indeed inescapable. It is this very framework which is destructive of life at large as it diminishes variety and the integral unity of things, the very balance of living systems.

There is nothing wrong with the Promethean imperative. There is nothing wrong with Progress. The Promethean pursuit within the context of the Greek world view and Greek mythology was a form of Progress. But the Promethean thrust within the totally mechanistic world, governed by instrumental values, is quite another form of Progress. For here Progress is reduced to material progress, and the Promethean imperative, without its vector of transcendence, becomes merely the instrumental imperative.

Now, either we take evolution, man and morality seriously and acknowledge that thinkers such as Teilhard de Chardin are of supreme relevance, or we only pretend to take them seriously, and through our indolence and lack of vision allow moral nihilism and relativism to prevail (let us remember that instrumentalism in the realm of values is a formidable ally of moral nihilism and total relativism). If we take evolution seriously, and ourselves as a special link in it, then it follows that we embark on a mobilization of our deeper faculties and facilitate new visions.

Transcendence is a part of our Promethean heritage and thus of our moral heritage. To consider the meaning of human life apart from acts of transcendence of the past, and not directed towards further transcendence in the future, would be to void it of its essential content. And the same is surely true of the meaning of the process of evolution at large. Now, since man recapitulates and crowns the process of evolution, in-depth understanding of the nature of the human being is tantamount to an understanding of the fundamental structure of evolution itself. At this point Teilhard's conception of man as an unfolding chapter of evolution, leading always to the next chapter, is not only justified but compelling. Teilhard's opus, properly read, gives us a clue as to how to pick up the thread of our Promethean heritage in the post-technological world.

Karl Popper's great achievement has been to show that in

order to understand the nature of science we have to understand its growth, its dynamic and dialectical unfolding; we have to go beyond the mere products of science, its most recent theories or their *logical* reconstructions. The same is true of evolution: in order to understand its nature we have to go beyond its molecular structure and beyond its logical reconstruction as merely a scientific theory; we have to understand its growth, its dynamic unfolding, its dialectics, its transformations.

5 *The New Cosmology*

We are now ready to assemble the various clues and fragments which our discussion has generated and which are parts of the alternative cosmology, and state the alternative moral imperative. It should come as no surprise to the reader that these fragments of the alternative have always been with us. However, for more than one reason, we have been unable to focus our vision and see them in a proper perspective. Life continues through the stuff of which it is made. It would be foolishness to think that a novel paradigm of knowledge or of values could be created by *deus ex machina*. Even the most novel departures are rooted in old concepts and visions. Evolution goes on, new patterns *are* created. The process of transcendence continues.

Before we address ourselves to the new moral imperative, we need to clear our cosmological path. For if the scientific cosmology continues to hold us in its embrace, we shall be grounded and frustrated. We must no longer cherish the illusion that the scientific world view is still our salvation and, given a chance, will deliver us to a harmonious, humane and satisfactory realm. To put the matter in the words of Erwin Schroedinger: 'The scientific picture of the real world around me is very deficient. It gives a lot of factual information, puts all our experience in a magnificently consistent order, but is ghostly silent about all and sundry that really matters to us. It cannot tell us a word about red and blue, bitter and sweet, physical pain and physical delight; it knows nothing of beautiful and ugly, good or bad, God and eternity.'

Cosmology in the image of mechanistic science, however, still holds us in its powerful embrace, and so-called common sense has been profoundly influenced by the Newtonian conception of the world. The conception of the universe as a factory is behind the pursuit of material progress, of instrumental values, of the ideology of consumerism. But curiously enough, this conception is much less prevalent, if it is held seriously at all, at the frontiers of science today. For those frontiers have now moved into sub-atomic physics, quantum theory, and the recognition that, in the last analysis, observer and observed merge. All these fresh extensions of science fundamentally alter and indeed undermine the static, deterministic, mechanistic view of the universe bequeathed to us by Newton. Yet so far they have been acknowledged neither in the workings of our common sense nor, indeed, in our conception of scientific method.

We have a truly paradoxical situation, then: modern science does not lend much support to what is popularly called the scientific-technological world view. Yet this world view, although it has been critically undermined by science itself, is powerfully sustained by a variety of institutions, including present schools and academia. What is it, then, that gives this world view its legitimacy and sustaining force? Above all, our ideals of secular salvation, which have generated a profusion of socio-economic institutions, including the motor industry and our habits of conspicuous consumption.

We often adhere to this world view because we feel that we must not betray the ideals of humanism. So much has been built and vested in this world view (the tradition of the

Enlightenment, the tradition of *Liberté, Egalité, Fraternité*) that we find it almost sacrilegious to question it seriously. We forget, at the same time, that the consequences of this world view, in the second half of the twentieth century, increasingly violate humanism, enlightenment, and liberty.

Science itself, and the research in and outside the laboratories of science, which is a part of our knowledge in the large sense, are continually undermining this scientific cosmology and providing the elements of the alternative. The subatomic physics of the last sixty years is not just an *addition* to Newtonian physics. It fundamentally alters the *picture* of our knowledge of the physical universe – that is, regarding its deterministic nature, its knowability, its ultimate components, its stability in terms of the constancy of its space-time frame. J. B. S. Haldane had the courage to say, 'The universe may not only be queerer than we suppose; it may be queerer than we *can* suppose.' The theoretical physicist, Dr. Evan Harris Walker, has said, 'It now appears that research under way offers the possibility of establishing the existence of an agency having the properties and characteristics ascribed to the religious concept of God.' The universe is again becoming a mysterious, fascinating place. Not only evolutionary biologists, but also astro-physicists have been providing impressive insights and arguments showing that evolution – leading to the evolution of man has not been a haphazard process. We are not just the result of blind permutations. Evolution has not been the stupid monkey that sits at the typewriter and, given infinite time, types out Shakespearean tragedies. Evolution has been something else – an exquisite series of compelling and mysterious transformations and transcendences. And this series, so it seems now, has required and necessitated the particular structure and characteristics that we find in the universe.

We are infinitely small as physical bodies. The universe is infinitely immense in its physical dimensions. Yet we needed this immensity as the laboratory to become what we are. Or rather, evolution needed this immensity and the particular density of matter, by and large homogeneous throughout the universe, and the burning of the stars, to carry on the process to the level of the human mind. For if the universe were not homogeneous in its density, then large parts of it would become so dense that they would have already undergone gravitational collapse. Other parts would have been so thin, John Archibald Wheeler[5] argues, that they would not be able to give birth to stars and galaxies. But this is not the end of the story. Why is the universe as large as it is? Why does it contain a number of particles which, according to our estimates, is about 10^{80}? And why has it existed for the length of time it has? The answer to all these questions is: in order to enable life to evolve. Now, in order to have life, we have to have elements heavier than hydrogen,[6] 'for no mechanism for life has ever been conceived that does not require elements heavier than hydrogen.' In order to obtain heavier atoms from hydrogen, thermonuclear combustion must take place. But thermonuclear combustion 'requires several billion years of cooking time in the interior of a star'. However, in order to be several billion years 'old', the universe has to be, according to general relativity, several billion light-years in extent. So why the bigness and the composition of the universe as it is? 'Because we are here!' This is, incidentally, the conclusion of the astro-physicist Wheeler himself.[7] We arrive, then, at an altogether new cosmology, which is not God-centred (as in the Bible), which is not man-centred (as in traditional humanism), which is not matter-centred (as in the dying scientific-technological world view), but which is evolution-centred.

Within the new cosmology, we receive an altogether new perspective on the universe, man and values.

The *universe* is here conceived of as evolving, mysterious, complex and exceedingly subtle in its operation. It is governed by physical laws in its segments of space-time, but these laws reflect only some aspects of its behavior. The universe is partly knowable, but what unfathomable mysteries it may still hold can hardly be imagined. A variety of systems of knowledge can be accepted, as none uniquely expresses all the content of the universe. Life is as much a part of it and an essential characteristic, as is matter, stars and galaxies. In order to understand its most important characteristics, we have to understand its evolution. This evolution has worked out toward more and more complex and hierarchical structures, culminating in biological organisms and finally in man. The universe is to be conceived of as home for man. We are not insignificant dust residing in one obscure corner of the universe; we are a cause, or at least a result of a most spectacular process in which all the forces of the universe have cooperated. This is at once a dazzling and a humbling prospect. For we are the custodians of the whole of evolution, and at the same time only the point on the arrow of evolution. We should feel comfortable in this universe, for we are not an anomaly, but its crowning glory. We are not lost in it, or alienated from it, for *it is us*. The Copernican revolution did not signify the estrangement of man from the world. *De Revolutionibus* is a hymn to the divine man in the divine cosmos. Only later, when the prophets of shallow materialism started to mold the course of our civilization, did man become 'reduced', and the Copernican revolution perverted. If we look at the matter clearly and carefully we find there is *nothing* in the entire corpus of physics, Newtonian physics especially, that prevents our viewing the universe as home for man, in the sense here discussed. It is rather our narrow vision and ill-conceived ideals that caused us to *read* into this physics the passing of transcendent man.

Man (within the new cosmology) is regarded as of the utmost importance, not in his own right, but as a shining particle of the unfolding process of evolution. The origins of Man may be in the cosmic dust, but during the billions of years of its transformations, evolution has produced such intricate, subtle and marvellous structures that the final product is nothing short of miraculous. Insofar as we embody, maintain, and attempt to refine this exquisite organization, we are the miraculous, we are the sacred. The sacredness of man is the uniqueness of his biological constitution which is endowed with such refined potentials that it can attain spirituality. The sacredness of man is his conscious awareness of his spirituality and his inner compulsion to maintain it. The sacredness of man is the awareness of the enormous respon-sibility for the outcome of evolution, the evolution which has culminated in us but which has to be carried on. Man is, in a sense, only a vessel, but vested with such powers and responsibilities that he is a sacred vessel.

Our uniqueness does not stem from being separated from it all nor from 'being the measure of all things in our own right', as traditional humanists have maintained, but from beholding the most precious characteristics worked out by life at large, from being the custodians of the treasury of evolution. We have lost some of the grandeur and glory attributed to man by older humanist conceptions. But we have gained something of inestimable value: we now form a unity with the rest of the cosmos, we are no longer alienated from it, we are a part of the cycle, woven into the rest; and the rest is woven into us: brute atoms and half-conscious cells have co-operated in order to bring us about.

Unity with the rest does not mean stagnation or dissolution into the primordial matter. Far from it; for there is nothing tranquil in this unity. Evolution has been a Promethean drama through and through, filled with sacrifice and hubris. Our life has happened as the result of innumerable acts of transcendence, some of which were steeped in blood and sacrifice. *We give meaning to our life while attempting to transcend it.* Such is the story of preconscious life. And such is the story of life endowed with self-consciousness. This conception of the meaning of life makes perfect sense for the pre-human forms of life and for human forms of life, be it high art or mundane day-to-day activity in which we want to get on with life, but 'a little bit better'. In each of these domains, we create meaning not by accepting the given, but by trying to transcend it. By the time man arrived, this universe was in the process of continuous transcendence, which we must continue, if only in order to exist.

Values (in our new cosmology) regulate man-to-man relationships; they also regulate man-to-life relationships. Values are neither God-centred nor merely man-centred, but evolution-centred. In the ultimate sense, we might say that human values, the values to live by in the human universe, which includes much more than human beings, are to be related to and derived from the process of the unfolding cosmos, for this cosmos, as we have argued, is a co-defining component of man in his evolution. Alternatively, we could say that these values are to be related to and derived from the structure of unfolding evolution. One has to be careful in saying that values are evolution-centred, to be derived from the structure of evolution, for much depends on the meaning one attaches to the term 'evolution'. If evolution is conceived of as a process of blind permutations, happening in the pre-eminently physico-chemical universe, then, at worst, evolution-centred values may mean the sanctification of the brutal and merciless in the name of the survival of the fittest; and, at best, they may mean a worship of inanimate nature. However, if evolution is conceived of as a humanization and spiritualization of primordial matters,[8] then the meaning of evolution in human terms spells out the meaning of human values. For values are those most refined aspects of human awareness, human dispositions and human aspirations which have made life extra-biological, which have made it spiritual, which have made it human.

The sanctity of values stems from our recognition, appreciation, indeed worship of those very characteristics of life, and the structures and hierarchies that support them, which have made life glowing in human terms. To live the life of a human being is to entertain sacredness and participate in sacredness, both of which, however, are given to us only potentially. One has to strive and labor, sometimes in great pain, to actualize this potential.

Within the New Cosmology, we recognize man as a part of and an extension of the evolving cosmos. This evolution enables us to attribute sanctity to man. His evolution-rooted sanctity makes man free of the tyranny of absolutes, in which earlier forms of sanctity were bound and, at the same time, allows him to transcend moral nihilism and relativism, with its arbitrariness and lawlessness.

6 *The New Imperative*

We do not wish to make a God of Biology, of Evolution, of Nature. Man's values are specifically and inherently human attributes. They must be expressed in human terms, that is, terms that have a comprehensive connotation for us on a variety of levels, which touch our minds, our hearts, and our bones. These values, indeed, embody, incorporate and crystallize the variety of forms of past evolution. Although, on the one hand, a product of a process and, on the other, a transitory stage, as we go on with our evolution to higher forms, these values must be considered as the unique set of man's characteristics, man's existential anchor. They should summarize the various phases of evolution but also, and above all, be guidelines for concrete human behavior: the principles which give meaning to human lives as lived in the universe which is both human and supra-human.

How should we look at these values which, on the one

hand, are the summation of the sensitivity of evolution and, on the other, concrete guidelines for human behavior in *this* world? What is our New Moral Imperative?

– behave in such a way as to preserve and enhance the unfolding of evolution and all its riches;
– behave in such a way as to preserve and enhance life, which is a necessary condition for carrying on evolution;
– behave in such a way as to preserve and enhance the eco-system, which is a necessary condition for further enhancement of life and consciousness;
– behave in such a way as to preserve and enhance the capacities which are the highest developed form of the evolved universe: consciousness, creativeness, compassion;
– behave in such a way as to preserve and enhance human life which is the vessel in which the most precious achievements of evolution are bestowed.

These five characteristics of the New Imperative are only variations on the same theme. They all follow from the first formulation. This is not only inevitable, but highly desirable. A moral imperative must be general enough to provide a philosophical foundation for values. But it must be fruitful and open-ended enough to generate specific consequences and guidelines for action. For ultimately, we have to relate it to specific actions and undertakings in our day-to-day living; and also we must be able to derive from it the criteria for rejection of other sets of values which are incompatible with our own.

We have discussed some moral imperatives of the past, not in order to show that they are all spurious, but rather to demonstrate that they were groping attempts in the right direction. Indeed, the vital core of some of these imperatives can be accommodated in our New Imperatives. If we were to employ the categories and concepts of the older imperatives, we might express the content of the New Imperative in the following way:

THE NEW IMPERATIVE
(comprises the following)

I *The Promethean Imperative:*
or the necessity for transcendence.

II *The Kantian Imperative:*
or the celebration of evolution's highest achievements.

III *The Ecological Imperative:*
or the necessity to preserve and enhance the living habitat around us.

From this New Imperative, we must sharply distinguish:

The Instrumental Imperative
(which is the Promethean imperative emptied of its transcendence).

The Technological Imperative
(which is the instrumental imperative carried to its logical conclusion: the instrument, the Machine dictates the modes of human behavior).

This presentation makes it immediately clear which part of our tradition we want to incorporate and why; and which part of our tradition we want to disinherit and why. I will now discuss the five imperatives in their turn, as they are related to our New Imperative.

The Promethean component of our New Imperative insists that the desire to improve, perfect and transcend our condition is inherently woven into the fabric of our life, is a *moral*

urge with which we are endowed. We cannot understand life
unfolding, human life especially, if we do not perceive that
to go beyond – whatever the stage of our accomplishment –
is in the very nature of life. In this sense, progress is not only
justified, but inevitable. But it is progress towards an ever
increasing transcendence and perfection. This progress towards ever increasing perfection cannot, on the level of
human life, be separated from the attainment and enhancement of spirituality.

Thus, all progress is spiritual progress. But, as the Promethean story shows, the way to progress is paved with
sacrifice, and sometimes ends with hubris. Insofar as we
sacrifice ourselves, consciously and unconsciously, we make
ourselves instruments for the attainment of other goals. The
story of evolution is a story of this kind of self sacrifice. Each
stage of evolution has made itself a means, an instrument
towards achieving the next stage. And it is the same in human
life. Sacrifice, selflessness and devotion are both natural and
inevitable.

Altruism is a part of our nature, a part of the human instinct. To recognize oneself as human is to recognize one's
capacity for altruism.[9] Societies which suppress altruism as a
mode of social behavior end up torn with strife, like our
present society. Moreover, altruism is an *essential* part of the
nature of evolution. Evolution would have long ago come to
a halt if it were not endowed with altruism as its *modus
operandi*. This truth is being slowly recognized by the most
recent research in biology and sociobiology. Edward Wilson
persuasively demonstrates, in his *Sociobiology: The New
Synthesis*, that there are forms of behavior to be seen among
bees, ants, baboons and other species which, from the human
point of view, must be recognized as altruistic. However,
Wilson undermines this thesis and his examples by attempting to find 'a more conventional biological explanation' for
this behavior; that is, the explanation which avoids any use

of transcendence. But evolution *is* a process of transcendence. One does not even begin to understand what 'altruistic behavior' might mean, if one is confined to conventional biological explanation. What may appear as idealism in human terms (altruism) is stark realism in evolution's terms. The basis of altruism is co-operation. Evolution without co-operation of its component parts would be null and void.

Seen in its evolutionary splendor, human life is a self-burning torch. We make countless sacrifices because we think it is worth it. We make instruments of ourselves because we consider the cause worthwhile. The Promethean aspects of our life, even when we sacrifice ourselves and burn ourselves out, are often intensely satisfying to the individual – take the lonely explorer who dies for the sake of Learning, Enlightenment, Mankind. These sacrifices are intensely satisfying because they are in harmony with the overall imperative: to preserve and enhance what is best in the species. The Promethean dimension of human life is contained in the process of ascription of meaning to life: 'We give meaning to our life while attempting to transcend it.'

But human life must never be turned into a means only. No cause is grand enough to require human sacrifice if, in the process, the human being does not fulfil himself as *human*. Hence the importance of the second part of our imperative, the Kantian Imperative: treat the life of every human being as an end in itself. Expressed in evolutionary terms, this second component of our New Imperative signifies the celebration of life at its present highest point. In its course, evolution creates such wonders ('What a piece of work is a man!') that to be truly aware of it, is to treat man as sacred. To live the life of a human being is to entertain sacredness and participate in sacredness. At this stage of evolution, man is an ultimate value. Yet we do not set him apart or treat him as a 'thing in itself', but in him we humbly acknowledge the workings of evolution. In this acknowledgment there is a tacit premise that evolution will go on, and that man can and will transcend himself and his present status. In this acknowledgment there is also a silent consent to allow man to turn himself into an instrument for the sake of the future, for the sake of the increased perfection of the species, and evolution at large. The dialectic between the means and the ends of human life is then painful and not easily reconcilable. In the ultimate analysis, we must never require a sacrifice from the individual for the sake of 'the future' if the individual does not fulfil his human destiny in the process. For, as we have argued, we may make ourselves into instruments, while at the same time fulfilling a part of our human destiny. We can be both ends and means at the same time. What is inadmissible is to turn human beings into *mere* means as has been done in totalitarian regimes, both ancient and recent. Here the Kantian aspect of our Imperative speaks with its full resounding voice.

We make sense of the Kantian Imperative, and incorporate it into our New Imperative, by giving it a new evolutionary meaning. Kant did not have our cosmological insight. In order to assure the sovereignty of the human person, he felt compelled to separate the human world from the physical world and then to invent 'things in themselves'. We can retain the sovereignty of the human individual while regarding him at the same time as a part of the evolving universe. Kant's Imperative is clearly an aspect of our New Imperative: in enshrining the human being, we are preserving and enhancing evolution's most accomplished creation. So-called 'inalienable rights' of the individual, which are sometimes tied to the Kantian Imperative, are not only in harmony with our Imperative, but clearly follow from it. Indeed, these 'rights' have a much more congruent and potent justification within our Imperative than within the framework of individualism or any other situational ethics.

Human life cannot be nurtured, nursed and sustained

unless we nurse and sustain the ecological habitat within the womb of which we all reside. Hence the importance of the third component of our new imperative -- the Ecological Imperative. We are at one with the ecological habitat for it represents the forms of life of which we are a part. There is a significant difference, however, between the two propositions: 'We have to take care of the ecological habitat because it feeds us,' on the one hand, and on the other, 'We have to take care of the ecological habitat because it is a part of us and we are a part of it.' In the former case 'we' and 'it' are apart, and 'it' serves 'us'. An instrumental attitude is visibly at work here, which is to say we treat the eco-system as a means, or a resource. In the latter case, 'we' and 'it' are one, and this is a necessity of a symbiotic and holistic attitude.

If human life is to be treated with reverence, so is the life of the ecological habitat. The ecological habitat is of intrinsic value, a part of life in general. At this point, Schweitzer's principle of 'Reverence for Life' must be reintroduced. We treat both human life and the ecological habitat with reverence – we treat them as intrinsic values because they represent very high achievements of the evolving universe. Schweitzer's imperative, needless to say, is congruent with our New Imperative. Yet the same phrase 'Reverence for Life' belongs to two different cosmologies and therefore has two different meanings. Within the Christian cosmology in which everything is God's personal property, the ethic based on 'Reverence for Life' at large is an anomaly. Within the New Cosmology, which considers the universe as home for man, the principle of Reverence for Life follows naturally.

Now, there will always be conflicts, clashes and agonies within the compass of life, for we cannot sustain all forms of life. Within the structure of evolution, the more highly developed the organism, the greater is its complexity and its sensitivity and the more reason to treat it as more valuable and precious than others. In a nutshell, the exquisiteness of man is more precious than the exquisiteness of the mosquito. In time of conflict, we care more for the life of a human being than the life of a mosquito. We have always known instinctively that the life of a human being is more valuable than the life of a mosquito. Our New Imperative gives a compelling reason why it should be so.

Thus we must take care of the ecological habitat, because it is an extension of our sensitivity. We are the guardians and stewards, not just 'users' of the eco-habitat in the same sense in which we are the guardians and stewards of human life and of our spiritual heritage. That is what the New Imperative means in terms of our ecological habitats and the evolving new eco-ethics.

Let us now take a closer look at the Instrumental and Technological Imperatives which have exerted a great deal of influence in our time, but which are *not* a part of our New Imperative. Instrumental values, as representative of the Instrumental Imperative, have their legitimacy in the Promethean Imperative. Indeed, they are derived from this imperative and in a sense are an aspect of it. For instrumental values represent an attempt to improve material conditions and thus indirectly the human condition. But the instrumental values of the Industrial Society have 'liberated' themselves from what is essential in the Promethean Imperative: the element of transcendence. (By transcendence we mean the augmentation and enhancement of our spirituality). Instrumental values are the ones that challenged the idea of hubris and themselves become the carriers of nemesis. They are derived from the Promethean Imperative, but they are outside our New Imperative, for in seizing on one aspect of our development, they simply forgot what this development is about. This is especially striking in the Technological Imperative which is a derivation of the Instrumental Imperative. The *raison d'être* of the Technological Imperative is *not* an enhancement of evolution at large, but an increase of industrial efficiency.

We have discussed the New Imperative in terms of older concepts and imperatives, but it would be inappropriate to think of it as a mere summation of older codes, or even as a synthesis of them. Synthesis belongs to the realm of chemistry. You can make it if you know in advance how to combine the various more primitive elements. World views and moral imperatives are not syntheses of this sort. They emerge out of human development as new species emerge in the course of evolution. None can be said to be a mere synthesis. They are more creations than combinations. Now, taking into account the intensity of our search for a non-relativistic ethic, and numerous attempts to rethink our cosmological predicament, it would appear that sooner or later someone would connect the two and show that ethics and cosmology co-define each other, or any rate complement each other, and that a non-relativistic ethic for the future would have to be rooted in a cosmology in which the universe is conceived of as Home for Man. It has been the chief purpose of this chapter to demonstrate just that. What seems to me unquestionable at this point is the fact that values can be derived from 'the laws of evolution'; but not in any obvious or trivial sense.

When the first amoebas transcended their original state of biological being and went on to something more complex and more refined, that was an act of true transcendence; yet not one that can be characterized as endowed with divinity. However, in the process of evolution, matter went on refining itself, its sensitivity and potentiality, to the point where it created man, who in his strivings and in his actualization of the potential given to him, engages in acts of transcendence which can be characterized as carrying with them spirituality and divinity.

Sacredness is acquired in the course of evolution, not given to us on a silver platter by an omnipotent and benevolent

God. Spirituality, sacredness and divinity are singular attributes of one chapter of evolution (Man), and these attributes
have been won through many tortuous and sometimes un-
believable biological, cognitive and spiritual battles – for the
original bio-chemical equipment of man did not particularly
favor the development of spirituality in us.

We are fragments of divinity in *status nascendi*. Spirituality
and divinity appear at the end of the process of spiritualization of matter, not at the beginning. We are actualizing God,
and we are bringing him to being, so to speak, by actualizing
the sensitivity-sacredness-divinity latent in us. God is at the
end of the road. We are its awkward, dim, unpolished fragments for the time being.

Transcendence without God *a priori* is possible, for transcendence stands for an ever-increasing perfection of our
capacities and attainments. Indeed only this concept of
transcendence is justified within a truly evolutionary perspective: transcendence that is void of an original God. If we
assume God at the beginning, then transcendence stands for
a process of curious retardation – of going back – and not for
the process of going beyond, and beyond, and beyond until
we reach pure spirituality.

Ecological humanism maintains that *we* are the universe
in the making. We strive for meaning through our own existential efforts. We give meaning to the universe through our
acquired humanity. We evolve aesthetic sensitivity as a part
of the evolutionary process. We acquire Mind and its various
cognitive capacities through our (and Evolution's) strivings.
We acquire spirituality as the result of our evolutionary unfolding. We acquire godliness by making gods of ourselves at
the end of our evolutionary journey.

Is the programme of Ecological Humanism so ambitious
as to be unrealistic? The 'realism' of our present thinking is
hopelessly *unrealistic*. Ecological Humanism cannot be proved

by argument but must be incorporated in the structure of our lives. I believe it has already been incorporated in various places, sometimes consciously, usually subconsciously, into existing ways of life. So in a sense I have merely attempted to grasp and codify the emerging new shapes of life. Above all, I have attempted to demonstrate that Ecological Humanism is a coherent philosophy, that it does not defy reason, for it is itself an expression of reason, of reason seen in its evolutionary unfolding.

Immanuel Kant asked: 'What is man?' His intention was not to describe human nature as it is, as it can be found by empirical surveys, but rather to discover the full scope of human potential.

Goethe said, as if answering Kant's question:

'To treat man as he is, is to debase him;
'To treat man as he ought to be, is to engrace him'.

To fulfil human potential is to transcend our present condition, to fulfil the requirement of evolution, to adapt the idiom of frugality which is a precondition of inner beauty, and to assure our short-term and long-term survival. Our immediate and long-term biological and environmental survival depends entirely on our capacity to remake the world from within. Transcendental-evolutionary values are nowadays an expression of historical necessity. To reach beyond is the evolutionary imperative, and it is the imperative of our present condition. Moreover, we have to reach beyond in order not to be swept away from where we are. The transcendant and the urgent are one. As Browning said:

'Ah, but a man's reach should exceed his grasp,
'Or what's a heaven for?'

NOTES

1. Although in the Communist countries the euphoria of Technology Triumphant still prevails, new voices of ecological consciousness, and of concern with larger things than technological progress, are being heard. Some are quite attuned to the ideals of Ecological Humanism here advocated. The Polish writer Julian Aleksandrowicz writes, in an essay significantly entitled 'The Ecological Conscience', as follows: 'Knowledge in the field of the humanities, particularly ethics, should not merely catch up with the technological sciences but overtake them. What can save us is an *ethical revolution* encompassing the entire international community. One of its basic conditions, indispensable for the protection of man against the accumulating trends of civilization's diseases, will therefore be the awakening, among young and adults, of an *ecological conscience* as (an) imperative for the protection of our psychosocial and biophysical environment, in order consciously to improve the 'quality of life' so essential for our health.' (*The Polish Perspectives*, January 1974).

2. Immanuel Kant, *The Groundwork of the Metaphysics of Morals*, II 67, Paton's translation, p. 96.

3. See especially Karl Popper's *Conjectures and Refutations*. It should be mentioned at this point that although piercing in his critique of logical positivism, Popper was a *positivist* (in the broad sense of the term) himself; he sought solutions to all our dilemmas in cognition alone; his intellectual universe seems to be limited to cognition alone—a typically positivist limitation.

4. Theodosius Dobzhansky, 'Advancement and Obsolescence in Science' in *Great Ideas Today, A Symposium on Tradition*, 1974, pp. 59 and 60.

5. John Archibald Wheeler, 'The Universe as Home for Man', *American Scientist*, Nov–Dec, 1974, p. 688 and ff.

6. Wheeler, *op. cit.* R. H. Dicke, *Nature*, 192, 1961, pp. 440–41.

7. Wheeler, *op. cit.*, p. 689.

8. Paolo Soleri, who in a creative way, carries on some of the ideas, one might even say the bulk of the ideas, of Teilhard de Chardin (see H. Skolimowski: 'Teilhard, Soleri and Evolution', *The Teilhard Review*, 3, 1975) has developed this theme in his *Matter Becoming Spirit*, 1973; and, of course, his idea of Arcology is an attempt to help this process of 'humanization'.

9. All those theories of aggression which revel in the apparently destructive nature of man and which are purportedly based on evolution, seem to be quite oblivious to the work evolution has done through its altruism. It is not asserted here that aggression is not part of our heritage, but *only* that altruism has prevailed and will prevail, because it is in the nature of evolution. We could not live one single day, even in the meanist of societies, without altruistic behavior occurring all the time.

4

Architecture and Eco-Philosophy

THEORY and practice are intimately connected. Immanuel Kant said that theory without practice is impotent and practice without theory is blind. Much of our present practice is blind because it is not informed by theory or rests on non-viable theory. The fusion of theory and practice is particularly striking in architecture. Architecture constitutes a bridge between logos and praxis; it is a point at which the two meet. For this reason architecture *visibly* demonstrates the greatness of our visions and equally the failure of our larger conceptions. In architecture, in brief, many of the ideas discussed in previous chapters find a visible embodiment.

The architecture inspired by the mechanistic logos has demonstrably failed us. The deficiencies of present architecture and its inability to shelter us adequately and to provide spaces that are life-enhancing is not so much the fault of architects and builders, but the fault of those larger conceptions on which architecture and our culture are based. It is at this level of analysis that the relevance of eco-philosophy is second to none: for it helps to understand in depth the deficiencies of present architecture and it indirectly provides a new foundation for architecture and the design process. In this chapter I will argue that the road to the improvement of architecture, indeed of total built environment, is not *via* new techniques and materials, but *via* new thinking, new assumptions, on which new architectural thinking will be based. We have to change our logos so that our practice is not

blind or counter-productive – either in architecture or elsewhere. Architecture, indeed, should be seen as a symbol of the
multitude of all other activities in which counter-productive
practice is a result of the mistaken logos.

1 *Form Follows Culture*

Architecture recapitulates culture, of which it is a part. In a
flourishing culture, architecture partakes in the glory. It then
expresses not only firmness and commodity but also delight.
When a culture is decaying and unable to sustain its idiom,
architecture comes in for much of the blame because its
shortcomings are strikingly visible and experienced by all.
While other social and political institutions, including educa-
tional ones, can more readily camouflage the malaise of the
culture which is expressed through them, architecture con-
spicuously reflects both triumphs and shadows.

The shadows of twentieth-century architecture are now
very conspicuous – so much so that society is alarmed by
them and architects are themselves deeply disturbed by the
state of affairs. To heap scurrilous abuse on the products of
contemporary architecture is as easy as it is futile.

Now, while it is a cliché to say that society has the kind of
architecture it deserves, it may be less of a cliché to maintain
that society has the kind of *culture* it deserves. And it may not
be a cliché at all to suggest that there is an intimate correla-
tion between architecture and culture, that, in general, architecture is a function of the dominant culture. At times, on the
other hand, architecture significantly articulates and helps to
define general culture. This dependence of architectural form
on the ethos of a given culture can be seen in all cultures,
including 'primitive' ones.

In the culture of the twentieth century, Western architecture is dominated by, and defined through, economics and

technology. If we look with a discerning eye at the variety of so-called new trends and tendencies, we cannot help observing that almost all of them are an expression of the technological ethos; epicycles of the technological system. Brutalism or Venturism, Archigram or rational architecture, operationalism or new rationalism – all bear the technological stamp. They are products of twentieth-century technological society. The Bauhaus (particularly in its classical period, when it became the dominant architectural ideology) epitomized the technological apologia. It found expression in the cult of efficiency and functionality, the belief in the machine and standardized norms, the worship of new materials and techniques. To these, all other aspects of architecture were to be subordinated.

It is not that we want to build sterile buildings, shoddy environments, spaces in which the human spirit is thwarted; our culture *makes* us design such environments and such spaces. There is something insidious in the spectacle of dedicated, determined and talented architects who can, and want to, build much better than they are allowed to or can afford to in the present context.

Building regulations and prohibitions have always existed. In the past they acted as filters through which the best of human imagination penetrated to produce the finest achievements. Now those filters have become so monumental that they do not let any imagination pass through; they allow no quality to emerge at the other end. This, of course, must produce a feeling of frustration, if not a slight schizophrenia, in the architects who utilize so much energy and imagination at *their* end and see so few positive results at the *other*. The best of their imagination is stuck in the filters and eliminated in the process.

Now, the power of those filters is not accidental; it is essential to the way in which the quantitative technological society works. It is not that we have incautiously multiplied codes and regulations, which are getting out of hand. It is rather that those codes and regulations guard and enforce the ethos of technological culture.

We have created a culture that systematically destroys quality. Those 'monumental filters', which interfere with our imagination and our desire to produce quality environments, are the culture's protective devices working to bar products which go against its quantitative ethos. Why do we then build inadequately? Because we have an inadequate culture. The culture is the filter.

Our growing ambivalence towards and sometimes outward rejection of planning is significant and symptomatic, not only because it demonstrates some important shifts in architectural theory and in articulation but also because it signifies important shifts in our culture. The rejection of planning is an implicit rejection of the linear, mechanistic, geometric, predominantly logical and economic mode of thinking and acting in favor of more organic, intuitive, decentralized, ecologically sound and life-enhancing forms. In changing our hearts and minds about planning, as a viable and necessary vehicle of architectural theory and practice, we simultaneously (although indirectly) change and re-articulate the idiom of our culture: away from its mechanized, objectivized matrix and towards one that accommodates and accentuates quality.

The architectural dogma of the first part of the twentieth century was: *form follows function*. When function became limited to its physical and economic parameters, we, as human beings, found the resultant form constraining and suffocating. So the slogan has been quietly dropped. 'Form follows function' was a specific articulation of technological culture within the realm of architecture. With hindsight we can now suggest a much more adequate characterization of architecture: *form follows culture*. Alternatively we could say: *shell recapitulates spirit* (i.e. as expressed by a given culture), or

even *shell accommodates spirit*. Thus, neither form follows function, nor shell before performance, but appropriate form to
accommodate the spirit of a culture. In short, *form follows
culture*.

Cultures always seek to vindicate their specific tenets and
achievements, even their obviously pathological traits. The
shortcomings of our own culture are painfully reflected in the
architecture of the recent past, which simultaneously signifies
a technological triumph and a human plight. That architecture constitutes clear evidence of the deficiencies of our
culture with its glorification of the objective, the physical,
and the efficient and its attempts to diminish the spiritual,
the sensitive, and the humane. In a nutshell, significant
changes in architecture are not going to be accomplished
either by introducing more efficient technologies or by simply
manipulating architectural theory. If we wish to change
architecture we cannot limit ourselves to architecture or
start with it alone. We have to start with – or simultaneously
address ourselves to – another level, the level of the general
culture that underlies the thinking and behavior of the age
we live in. That start has in fact been made, and we are
already changing the idiom of our culture and the idioms of
architecture and planning – away from the linear and pseudo-
rational and towards the ecological, the organic, the compassionate.

2   *Space and Life*

We live in *space*. The concept of space is both very easy to
grasp and very difficult to articulate. St. Augustine was once
asked, 'What is time?' He replied, 'I know when you do not
ask.' It is like that with the concept of space: we know what it
is, yet we have trouble putting it into words.

Needless, to say, architecture space, the kind of space

which we create while building human habitats, and while interacting in them in a variety of human ways, is different from merely physical space. And here is the crux of the matter. Within the technological system – and its imperatives of objectivization, quantification and standardization – we have reduced the variety of spaces to purely physical, Newtonian space. Being only dimly aware of this, we have been forced to design Newtonian space, which recognizes extent and volume but does not recognize non-physical qualities and attributes.

The concept of technological space is a variant of Newtonian space. Technological space attempts to arrange environments according to the dictates and demands of the industrial system and efficiency. Major environmental and social calamities have occurred in recent times because we have uncritically accepted technological space as the basis of our design activities. The limitations of technological space are obvious to anybody who stops to reflect upon its characteristics. But only recently have we allowed ourselves the luxury of such a reflection. As a result, we have re-introduced into the language of architecture other aspects of human space: social, psychological and aesthetic. These are sometimes covered by one name – *existential space.*

Recognition of the social, psychological, aesthetic and spiritual aspects of human space is nothing new. The builders of the Gothic cathedrals were living embodiments of this recognition. But we need not go back so far; we can see this recognition explicitly expressed in our own day among the American Indians, particularly the Plains Indians.

Black Elk Speaks is a moving account of the last days of the Oglala tribe of the Sioux nation. Black Elk is a holy man of the Sioux. When he bemoans the destruction of his people, he refers not only to the physical extermination of the Sioux nation, but also to the destruction of the space that was so important to the well-being of his people. The circle was the sacred shape in the Sioux system of beliefs. 'The life of man,' says Black Elk, 'is a circle from childhood to childhood and so it is in everything where power moves. Our teepees were round like the nests of birds and these were always set in a circle, the nation's hoop, a nest of many nests, where the great white spirit meant for us to hatch our children. But the Wasichus (Whitemen) have put us in these square boxes. Our power is gone and we are dying, for the power is not in us any more. You can look at our boys and see how it is with us. When we were living by the power of the circle in the way we should, boys were men at thirteen years of age. But now it takes them very much longer to mature.'[1]

Whether we are willing to accept the mythology of the Sioux, or of the medieval masons for that matter, is of secondary importance. What is of primary importance is that we should realize that both medieval builders and the Sioux impregnated their conception of space with transphysical characteristics. This conception of space was an intrinsic part of their conception of man and of the world at large. *Man's conception of space is a function of his culture.*

In order to envisage and design spaces which satisfy the variety of human needs – with aesthetic and spiritual needs perhaps the most important – we may have to recognize the human being as sacred. We can perhaps say without exaggeration that it is within sacred space that the quality of life resides. Anyone who is allergic to the term 'sacred' because of its associations with past religions can use the term existential space to denote its peculiarly human qualities, its irreducible and specifically human content: aesthetic, spiritual and cultural.

Quality of life as a product of a person's interaction with his environment does not stand a chance in the sterile geometric spaces of modern architecture. Life does not like to be boxed. Life likes more amorphous, varied spaces. Our biological heritage is more attuned to nooks and crannies, the irregular and the round than to linear geometry. In actual experience we find linear cities and other habitats expressing the canons of geometric planning unsatisfactory, if not disturbing, because they do violence to our biological heritage, to the amorphous and irregular in us, which is the stuff of all organic life.

Architects and designers must not be afraid of the idea of Life, and the criterion of the quality of life. Architecture is about life. Our contemporary social rebellion against the sterility of modern architecture is an expression of these judgements of life. Since we cannot and should not avoid them, we must attempt to anticipate and meet them. Quality has become a prominent term in recent architectural discussions. The reintroduction of the concept is an acknowledgment that judgements of life are once more relevant to architecture.

3   *The Quest for Quality*

Quality is a difficult term to define, particularly in the context of the quantitative society. Moreover the idea of quality in architecture is by no means a simple one. The term can signify at least four different though inter-related things:

Q_I quality of design (the original idea and its representation on paper, i.e. the drawings).

Q_{II} quality of processes (the various means, techniques and technologies employed in the process of construction).

Q_{III} quality of products (the assessment of buildings upon their completion).

Q_{IV} the quality of life generated by built environments (the quality of people's interaction with environments).

It is, of course, the fourth level that is all-important because it ultimately redeems all the others. Ideally one would like to assume that quality on one level implied quality on the next, so that quality of design resulted in quality building, and ultimately in quality of life in the built environment. In the real world the relationships are not that simple. They are clearly asymmetrical. Quality at the first three levels: design, processes and building, does not automatically guarantee quality at the fourth level – the 'quality of life' of built environments. Thus the conjunction of Q_I, Q_{II} and Q_{III} does not automatically imply Q_{IV}. Let us put it in the form of a formula. (Bar over the letter means negation.)

(i) $(Q_I \cdot Q_{II} \cdot Q_{III} \cdot) \to Q_{IV}$.

There are other asymmetries. Q_I does not automatically secure either Q_{II} or Q_{III}.

(ii) $Q_I \to \overline{Q}_{II}$; $Q_I \to \overline{Q}_{III}$, and furthermore:

(iii) $(Q_I \cdot Q_{II}) \to \overline{Q}_{III}$

We can assess quality only *post hoc*, only *a posteriori*. If we find a given environment working, if it generates interactions which we deem to be life-enhancing, then we judge the building to be a success. Quality of life, Q_{IV} automatically implies Q_{III}.

(iv) $Q_{III} \leftarrow Q_{IV}$

A good example is the National Theater on London's South Bank. Although many have questioned the processes and the product, those cold, brute masses of concrete, the quality of life which the environment of the National Theater has generated is such that we have to consider the building a success. So, quality of life generated by built environments automatically secures all other qualities.

(v) $Q_I \nwarrow$
$Q_{II} \leftarrow \Big\{ Q_{IV}$
$Q_{III} \swarrow$

The quality of the final link, of the culminating point, determines the quality of the contributing links. There is another justification for this criterion of quality. In logic, there is a law called the retransmittability of falsity. If p implies q, $(p{\rightarrow}q)$, then it does not automatically follow that q implies p, $(q{\rightarrow}p)$. But it does follow that if not q, then not p, $(\bar{q}{\rightarrow}\bar{p})$; in short: $(p{\rightarrow}q){\rightarrow}(\bar{q}{\rightarrow}\bar{p})$. In other words, a negative judgement about the quality of life generated by a given environment (building) automatically retransmits that negative judgement to the contributing links Q_I, Q_{II}, Q_{III}, either to some of them or to all of them.

The *determining* practice and result is Q_{II}, quality of processes, for this is the particular quality which is favored by the technological system. Quality of processes can be subdivided into at least three sub-categories:

adequacy of technical means;
adequacy in meeting urban and planning requirements;
adequacy in meeting economic criteria.

The search for quality in our day is clear proof of the fact that we have not lost the sense of the concept and, moreover, that we are transcending the boundaries of technological culture. This search for quality can be seen in unlikely places. Robert Pirsig's book, *Zen and the Art of Motorcycle Maintenance*, is relevant to our discussion here: 'Any philosophic explanation of Quality is going to be both false and true precisely because it is a philosophical explanation. The process of philosophic explanation is an analytical process, a process of breaking something down into subjects and predicates. What I mean (and everybody else means) by the word quality cannot be broken down into subjects and predicates. This is not because Quality is so mysterious but because Quality is so simple, immediate and direct . . . Quality cannot be defined . . . If we define it we are defining something less than Quality itself.'[2]

Quality-of-life architecture is architecture which has the courage to recognize the spiritual and transcendental dimensions of the human beings. Quality resides in spaces which are deliberately and purposely endowed with characteristics and attributes which are transphysical. Physical well-being is not a physical state but a psychological one.

The two outstanding architects of the twentieth century, men who held life at the center of their vision and designed to meet the requirements of the radiance of human life, have been, in the first half of the century, Frank Lloyd Wright and, in the second half, Paolo Soleri. While Wright designed exquisite *individual* houses which blended organically with their environment, Soleri has designed whole cities, called 'arcologies (a fusion of architecture and ecology), which meet the challenge of the post-industrial era by attempting to blend man and nature in a novel way. Soleri's arcologies are monumental architectural designs for frugal, ecological living. At their center, however, lies the human imperative, which demands that, in addition to man's economic and physical needs, the desiderata of human life at its most developed cultural and spiritual levels shall also find full satisfaction. Soleri's exemplary achievement is to have expressed, in his arcologies, the architectural, the ecological, the frugal, and the spiritual.

In summary, the true purpose of architecture is to continue, enhance, and celebrate life. The phrase 'to continue, enhance, and celebrate life' must be seen in its proper context. The industrial sharks who destroy our ecological habitats for profit and often force architects to design anti-life environments can claim to be continuing, enhancing, and celebrating their own lives. Individual greed must not obscure from our view the fact that the eco-system urges various constraints upon us. In addition to our ecological awareness we must have a coherent conception of man and a viable model of culture that are capable of sustaining us in the long run.

If what I have said is correct then so-called people's architecture, that is an architecture designed not by architects but by lay people, has little legitimacy and even less merit, so long as the people are conditioned and manipulated to submit to their acquisitive instincts. In our lowbrow culture, which is so often proletarian in the worst sense, the architect must assert his role as a patrician, must lead instead of bowing to acquisitive and materialist preferences. Only when people transcend their obsession with material acquisitiveness – which is one of the chief causes of environmental destruction and of our inner emptiness – will it be time for the architect to relinquish his role as the designer of complete environments. This may be an unpopular suggestion, contravening as it does the ethos of egalitarianism. But have we not had enough mediocrity, environmental debacles and disasters to realize that the egalitarian ethos is not capable of designing, in this complex world, to meet quality-of-life criteria? For the egalitarian ethos (or the anti-élitist stance) too often tends to be standard, undistinguished, careless and morbid, thus ultimately leading to anti-quality spaces.

The re-orientation of our vision concerning priorities calls for a new idiom of architectural thinking and articulation. It also calls for a re-definition of the present idiom of culture. The new idioms of architectural articulation and of culture will parallel each other because they will be two different aspects of the same thing.

We are clearly groping towards a new paradigm in architecture. I use the term paradigm in the sense in which Thomas Kuhn uses it in *The Structure of Scientific Revolutions*: as an overall conceptual umbrella which includes assumptions, practices, theories, as well as criteria of judgement of finished products. By shifting the emphasis from technical virtuosity of means to the quality of life, we are changing not just a small part of practice; we are changing the whole idiom of architecture, we are changing the entire paradigm.

Traditionally, through millennia, architecture was defined by a context in which religion and art predominated.

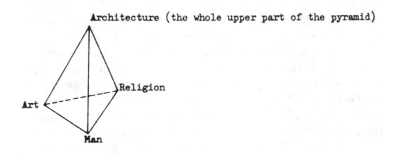

Architecture (the whole upper part of the pyramid)

In the nineteenth century, and particularly in the twentieth century, we changed the context and architecture came to be defined and determined by economics and technology.

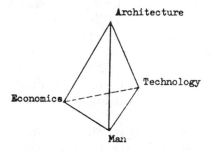

In both these respective periods the prevailing conception of man was a by-product of the prevailing culture.

We are now at the threshold of a new synthesis in which architecture is rooted in society and ecology. Let us be clearly aware that in the past, in the fifties and sixties, technological escapades dominated our thinking. We paid lip-service to so-called human concerns, while in fact architecture was increasingly rooted in technology and economics. Now the basis of architecture is radically enlarged.

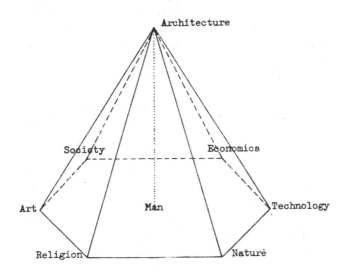

Our explicit recognition of the social and ecological as well as the religious contexts (by acknowledging the spiritual aspects of man's existence and designing spaces in which those aspects can be fulfilled), in addition to the technological and economic contexts, makes us look at architecture and design in an altogether new way. The new paradigm is in the making. This new paradigm is evolving around the new imperative that the true purpose of architecture is to continue, enhance and celebrate life. This imperative, as we can clearly see, is an extension of the ecological imperative we discussed in chapter 3. This is to be expected: if the ecological imperative is valid it should be applicable to a variety of fields. Architecture is one of them.

The quality-of-life criterion, which is the architectural formulation of the ecological imperative, has a number of specific and tangible consequences. Quality means breaking away from the tyranny of centralization, which is the tyranny of mediocrity. It calls for appropriate technologies, usually soft (for high-powered technologies invariably destroy the delicate tissue of quality). And it implies frugality and durability in the things we produce (the throw-away society is the arch-enemy of quality). In short, it signifies a whole new system of instrumentation, including a new attitude towards work – you cannot have a quality-of-life environment if human work is systematically degraded or reduced to stupifying, mechanical, repetitive tasks. These consequences of quality-of-life architecture are too fundamental to be accommodated within the confines of today's technological culture with its imperatives of objectivization, quantification and economic suboptimization.

How are all these changes to be brought about? The transition from any form of logos to daily practice is always a troublesome process. We may find that, before we can design and execute quality-of-life architecture, we shall have to adjust our political institutions.

The quality-of-life criterion is ultimately a political one. We may have to change our politicians and our social and political institutions before this criterion can prevail. We shall need people with superior judgement, at various levels of the political hierarchy, who can see that quality-of-life environments are not a luxury but a necessity: environmental, social, ecological, psychological, aesthetic and political.

Architecture has a great and salutary role to play in the future. Society expects architects to take care of the complete environment, for there is nobody else to do it. Architects cannot refuse this responsibility. In recent years they have gone half-way towards their destiny by designing new blueprints for alternative habitats, including new uses of solar energy and frugal management of scarce natural resources. In order to fulfil the social responsibility that is thrust upon them, architects must have the courage of their convictions, have to prevail with their quality criteria over mountains of paralysing regulations, and to be relentless and unbending in bringing architecture back to Life.

We must not blame everything on 'the system'. This would be too easy. We must see ourselves as a part of the equation. We must infuse ourselves with the spirit of innovation, inspiration, oneness with the environment and compassionate caring for others so that it shines through our designs and buildings and the system is transformed in our acts of creative transcendence.

NOTES

1. *Black Elk Speaks*, the life story of a Holy Man of the Oglala Sioux as told through John G. Neihardt (Flaming Rainbow), University of Nebraska Press, Lincoln, 1961.

2. Robert Pirsig, *Zen and the Art of Motorcycle Maintenance*, 1975, pp. 244 and 245.

5

Celebrating Life

1 *Religion as a Life Enhancing Phenomenon*

WE are a daring civilization. An adventurous civilization. But we are also a stupid civilization, afflicted with a death wish. We are destroying (not just using, but destroying) natural resources and habitats that are the very tissue from which society is made. We are destroying, by the increasing number and magnitude of various stresses, individual human beings. We are destroying life at large. The civilization which intentionally or unintentionally does all these things cannot be called either judicious or wise. But I do not intend, in this last chapter, to recite a catalog of our sins and follies or cast another prophecy of doom. I prefer to praise Life, with its extraordinary endowments and capacities of which we are a living embodiment.

We have behind us the whole heritage of life: life unfolding, developing, emerging into new forms. We are just one form of life. We are aware of uniqueness, and of our superiority over other forms of life. But this superiority is not so much *our* superiority as the superiority of nature, the superiority of life itself, which is capable of evolving selfconsciousness and capable of writing poetry – through us.

Life had evolved this extraordinary variety of forms not in order to be extinguished by one species intoxicated by its power, by one civilization gone topsy-turvy in its one-sided development. Life is stronger, more enduring, more cunning, more extraordinary than the cunning and extraordinariness of one of its species. I believe that life will prevail in spite of us, in spite of the death wish of our civilization.

Life will find an avenue to use us cunningly to its own ends. Sooner or later life in us will alter those destructive structures which threaten not only human societies but a larger heritage of evolution. Indirectly and cunningly our instinct for survival, or, to put it in more general terms, the genius of life to assert and perpetuate itself, will make us redesign the various social institutions which are nowadays incongruous, will make us relinquish our more parasitic practices, will make us give up many of our wants. We shall survive because life will survive, because life is stronger and more enduring than any of its species. This is not an expression of blind optimism about man's future, nor is it a declaration of the nobility of man and his ultimate goodness, but rather an expression of optimism about the future of Life. Life will guard its assets by protecting us even against ourselves. There is enough creative power and genius in life to do just that. Now, if anyone should insist that this conception of life is relentless and unfolding, enduring and creative, and suggest that life is God, we shall not protest too much.

We can think of life as mere chemistry. We can think of chemistry as mere physics. Consequently we can think of life as mere mechanistic interactions of physical bodies and chemical particles. And in so doing we are being 'scientific' and clearly obeying the criteria of instrumental rationality. But will this scientific thinking touch upon life as we live it? In short, we can cheapen and brutalize the meaning of human life by translating it into mere physio-chemical matrices. But we cannot escape the feeling that this is cheapening the meaning of life.

Because of its extraordinary creative capacities, bordering on the miraculous, life could be called 'divine'. To say this, however, is not to preach a return to traditional religions. Yet there are aspects of traditional religions which add something

significant to man's substance, and if rejected or neglected seem
to produce a crippling effect on man's life. Without worship,
man shrinks. If you worship nothing, you are nothing.

There are signs of a spiritual revival in many places and in
many forms. After decades of existential anguish, based on
the philosophy of nothingness, where the human being is aim-
lessly drifting through the meaningless universe, a desperately
lonely particle, we are beginning to look at the phenomenon
of man in a new way.

Traditional religions have articulated the structures of
man's need to worship ideals larger than himself. Those structures are often mystified and frequently distorted by practice
and ritual. The distortions and mystifications should not,
however, obscure from our view the fact that the primary
function of religious structures is to provide a framework for
ideals which are inspiring and sustaining to our life.

We invest our deities with the most illustrious attributes
we desire to possess, and then through the emulation of these
attributes we make something of ourselves: as human beings
and as spiritual beings. Our humanity is the product of our
mirroring in our lives the qualities we have vested in our
deities. The symbolic transformation of reality has been no
less significant in the ascent of humanized man than the in-
vention of tools and of language. The role of religion in this
symbolic transformation has been second to none. Religion
transforms reality with a view to making man unselfish and
altruistic; it inspires him with transcendental ideals which
help him to live within the human family and help to reconcile man with himself. This is a supreme and salutary aspect
of the traditional religions.

Religion, ultimately, is an instrument in man's search for
his identity, his integrity, in his painful struggles with himself
to attain and preserve his humanity and spirituality. Life has
created an arsenal of means and devices to enhance and perpetuate itself. On the level of human consciousness and

human culture, it has created art and religion as the instruments for safeguarding its highest accomplishments. Seen in a broader perspective, art and even language itself are instruments of self-articulating life.

We must not be overly impressed by the secondary aspects of religion, art or language. Specifically, we must not confine our attention to their pathological aspects but look at them as vehicles of the articulation and refinement of life at large.

When conceived as instruments of the perfectibility of man, worship and religion have positive functions. Infatuated with the ideal of material progress, we have forgotten the many salutary aspects of traditional religion. Euripides was right when he said:

'Who rightly with necessity complies,
In things divine we count him skilled and wise.'

Modern thinkers, such as Nietzsche, Marx, Engels, the Marxists and so many humanists of various denominations in our day have concentrated purely on the secondary and negative functions of religion. In denying religion, they have so often negated the spiritual heritage of mankind. In fighting against the last vestiges of traditional religion, Christianity in particular, they have inadvertently shrunk the meaning of man's existence by reducing it to his economic activity.

2 *Life is Knowledge*

There is an immense store of knowledge in us because we are alive and because we are an exquisite repository of life. We are continually steeped in our evolutionary heritage and we use the knowledge stored in us at times so cunningly and ingeniously that we cannot understand it. That is to say, we cannot understand 'it' through the categories of accepted knowledge; we cannot explain this understanding in the categories permitted by accepted knowledge. Yet deep down we do understand it. The epistemology of life has to be created. At present we only have epistemologies concerned with abstract underpinnings.

It is easier to postulate that life is knowledge and that life and knowledge are linked together than to explain it. We are ill-equipped to understand the epistemology of life in us and life around us because our understanding has been conditioned and determined by abstract understanding, by objective understanding, by scientific understanding. Objective understanding is a part of understanding at large, for nature has endowed us with minds and one of the attributes of the mind is that it can objectivize. Abstraction conceived of as a human faculty is not a monstrous aberration of the human mind; it is one of the modus operandi of life. But in addition to this aspect of understanding there are other aspects which require empathy as their modus operandi. We have less difficulty in *employing* empathy as a mode of understanding than in *justifying* it in our system of knowledge. We understand *via* empathy, but we cannot easily explain it when pressed to do so.

The laboratory of the world is contained in all of us. The entire chemistry of the cosmos is circulating in you. The chains of energy are transformed into life. How does it happen that energy is transformed into life? Two grammes of energy into one gram of life? What is this energy that becomes life? And then becomes consciousness? Or take the relationship between chemistry and consciousness – we all know that it exists. If we starve the brain of oxygen, loss of consciousness follows. But this is only a tiny facet of what is there, of what takes place. We must excavate the cognitive layers of our evolution!

We so often resort to the knowledge stored in the layers of our evolution, and on occasion we have an awareness of it too. The language of the body, the language of the skin, the language of the eyes – they all have their inner grammar. What would our life have been without those languages? When my eyes meet your eyes I know instantly who you are, even if I cannot express it, either to you or to myself. I walk through life avoiding those against whom my eyes have warned me; and casting an invisible net over those whom my eyes have approved. I have knowledge in my eyes, and I know it. When I look into your eyes, you are an open quarry to me, in which I can see all the shapes chiselled out by life.

I can understand you through my skin. I can catch the quivering of your biology through the sparks of your eyes. I can submerge myself in your being, because my being and your being have been molded by the same evolutionary forces and share the same heritage of life. Through my skin and tissues, through my senses and my mind acting in unison, I can tune in to listen to you and myself as to the music of evolution. My body, my skin, my eyes are the tentacles through which life rolls on, through which we tune in to the music of evolution, of which we are a part. To be rational is to understand the music of the spheres. To be truly rational is to combine and reconcile the rationality of the brain with the rationality of life; here lies the wisdom which transcends mere intellectual dexterity.

Is the poetry of my utterance the denial of the meaning of my words? Are things of beauty meaningless because not amenable to empirical verification? On the contrary, the function of beauty is the enhancement of the aesthetic and so of the biological aspects of life. *The function of poetry is a condensed symbolic articulation of life.* In the long run, research into the epistemology of life and into empathetic modes of understanding will be carried on and will be recorded in discursive treatises. Perhaps there will come a time when we shan't need discursive treatises, we shan't need the crutches of logic, for our understanding will be much swifter and much more

direct. At present this epistemology and this mode of understanding are cultivated and used by us individually and often
surreptitiously against the explicit dicta of discursive reason.

The epistemology of life signifies mapping out the terri-
tories of our implicit faculties and resources of knowledge,
including the subconscious, intuitive, and extrasensory,
which participate in our acts of perception and comprehension, which guide us through the labyrinth of actual living,
of which we are aware, if only dimly (and this dim awareness
will have to be articulated as part of the epistemology of life),
and which, in short, indelibly and uniquely determine the
modus of our life on various levels of being, and which also
determine the character of our interactions with other modes
of being. We must be aware that all of this happens beyond
the confines and criteria of our current empirically oriented,
discursive epistemologies. The first pre-condition for establishing an adequate epistemology of life is the recognition
that *the life process is a knowledge process*, that the knowledge of
the brain cannot be separated from the knowledge contained
in our elementary cells, that abstract knowledge is only one
end of the spectrum of which the other end is knowledge of
amoebas from which we grew and with which we remain (as
with everything else on the evolutionary ladder) in the
cellular-blood relationship as we breathe and beat with the
same rhythm of life. All forms of knowledge that we share
with other forms of life, and all prediscursive or trans-
discursive forms of cognition that are stored in the layers of
our being, I call biological knowledge.

My philosophical forerunners in the twentieth century are
Whitehead, Teilhard de Chardin, and Heidegger. On the
other side is the analytical tradition of Russell, Carnap and
Austin in which the refinement of language has been pursued
at the expence of our comprehension of larger philosophical
problems. It is this analytical tradition that still dominates
present-day acadmic philosophy, and it is this tradition that

Eco-philosophy opposes and seeks to replace. The epistemology of life is an articulation of Eco-philosophy. One of the tenets of Eco-philosophy is that it is committed to life. Being committed to life, it must understand life and this ultimately means that it must celebrate life, not in any outward and facile merry-making but in a deep, almost metaphysical awareness of the wonderfully complex and mysterious nature of life.

The plastic environment is one of the creations of the scholarly genius of the twentieth century. But we always escape back to nature. The natural environment is the stuff of which we are made. We are oppressed by plastic environments (if only subconsciously) because life there is extinguished. And we need life around us to feel that we are alive.

The elusive nature of life vis-à-vis science is beautifully described by Albert Szent Gyorgi, a Nobel Laureate:

> 'In my hunt for the secret of life, I started my research in histology. Unsatisfied by the information that cellular morphology could give me about life, I turned to physiology. Finding physiology too complex, I took up pharmacology. Still finding the situation too complicated, I turned to bacteriology. But bacteria were even too complex, so I descended to the molecular level, studying chemistry and physical chemistry. After twenty years work, I was led to conclude that to understand life we have to descend to the electronic level, and to the world of wave mechanics. But electrons are just electrons and have no life at all. Evidently on the way I lost life; it had run out between my fingers.'

Science is today the established orthodoxy. It commands the support of the majority of educated people; if for no other reason than because this educated majority has gone through the mill of a scientifically oriented education and has been simply conditioned, if not actually brainwashed, by the precepts of the scientific understanding. However, real progress is not made by loud, ostentatious, pushy majorities, scientific or otherwise. It is made by small and obstinate minorities. From time immemorial, when the first amoebas started to multiply themselves and gave birth to more complex organisms, the story of life has been the story of deviant minorities which, by not conforming to the established order of things, thereby evolved new characteristics and new functions. Progress on the evolutionary scale has always been achieved by tiny minorities inching their own way to produce new mutants, and ultimately new forms of life: genetic, biological, cultural, intellectual, spiritual. The poetry of life is inexhaustible. Life is not objective. Life is devouring. Life is self-transcending. The ferocious intensity of life's beat is the only rhythm worth listening to.

How this minority, which is questioning the omnipotence and omniscience of scientific-technological progress, is going to steer us into a life of sanity and alternative modes of interaction with nature and other human beings is still an open question. Martin Heidegger, at the end of his life and in a state of complete despair, maintained that only God can save us. This was no new option, relegating our responsibility to extrahuman agencies. We do not need a miracle. We need a concerted *will* to alter our own destiny. We need to cooperate with Life itself in getting over the ugly bump which our technological civilization has created, ostensibly to further progress. This bump is not the first of its kind. Similar ones have been overcome in the past. But not by mere inertia and through the indolent assumption that 'the genius of life will save us'. Our wisdom and determination are part of the genius of life.

We shall need to create new myths to make this transition possible. Two myths in the making are: the myth of the unity of the family of man within the context of the universal sympathy for all; and the myth maintaining that the cosmos is pervaded with spirituality, which leads to the realization that we are a part of a sacred tapestry. We shall need to create a new theology, for no world view is complete without a theology, even if it is an implicit one. Raimundo Panikarr is working along similar lines when he says: 'Curiously and significantly enough, this emerging myth [of the unity of mankind] seems to reverse the old myth of monogenism which located the unity of the human race in its unique origin. Nowadays the unity of mankind appears much less in the origin than in the finale.'

The new theology underlying Ecological Humanism is that we are God-in-the-process-of-becoming. We are fragments of grace and spirituality *in status nascendi*. We give testimony to our extraordinary (divine) potential by actualizing these fragments in us. By creating ourselves into radiant and spiritual beings, we are helping to create God-in-the-process-of-becoming, which is our own becoming. God and our divinity are at the end of our road, at the end of time, at the end of mankind, in the finale. Our task is to become fully aware that, as the result of certain propensities of unfolding evolution, we possess the potential for making ourselves into spiritual beings, and thereby bring to fruition some of the seeds of God in the process of self-making. This *ecological theology* provides not only a new cosmological scheme; it also has an existential import: it brings into sharp focus the meaning of our individual life, which is redeemed in so far as we elicit from ourselves our potential godliness. This theology also justifies the emerging myth of the unity of the human family: we are all striving towards the actualization of something much greater than our individual selves, something that transcends the boundaries of all states and all cultures.

There is no way of demonstrating the truth of the myths which will be actualized at the end of time. But there is no way of demonstrating their falsity either. The value and viability of myths is to be judged by the inspiration they provide and the sustaining power they can generate. The eschatology of atheism has exhausted itself. We have nowhere to go within the deterministic boxes of the mechanistic universe. If we are to go anywhere beyond our present condition, we must have the universe open to us once again: not as an empty road leading to nothingness but as a journey leading to increasing consummation of our spiritual potential.

Life will prevail because it is stronger than any of its particular manifestations. Having articulated itself into awareness and enlightenment, of which we human beings are for the time being the guardians and custodians, it will not allow itself to be pushed to its lower levels. There is more to life than organic matter and its living processes. The inventiveness of nature is a part of its modus operandi. The genius of nature is an intrinsic aspect of its development. No organism or form of life relinquishes achievements and capacities which it has evolved in the course of its evolution. And this is also true of life at large. It will guard its inventiveness and genius for these are its most precious assets, and inherent modalities of its existence.

The cunning of life is infinite. For cunning is one of the devices through which the inventiveness of life and its march forward can be assured. Life uses us and all its other offsprings to perpetuate itself. Whether this is anthropomorphizing life is beside the point. If this approach is called metaphysics, so be it. Life is certainly beyond physics, and this is exactly what the term metaphysics means – beyond physics. If the genius of life is removed from us, what is left of us? A Skinnerian pigeon? The pigeon is a marvel of the inventiveness of nature. To understand the pigeon alone is to accept the metaphysics of life.

Life and evolution are one. To understand life, we have to understand evolution. To understand evolution, we have to understand life. The knowledge of evolution is the beginning of wisdom. To submit to evolution and the flow of life is not resignation and slavery but an enlightenment and a deeper comprehension of the human condition. In our understanding of the infinite riches and capacities of life, we are only toddlers.

We shall learn how to manage the subtleties of life unfolding because life will use us for this purpose. We shall learn the epistemology of life. We shall learn the awesome responsibility of accepting ourselves as fragments of God in the process of becoming. It is a glorious contingency that out of dimness may emerge radiance. We should not bemoan the fact that we are an instrument of life perfecting itself and perpetuating itself through us, for we do not have any other choice. Above all we must try to understand that this is in the nature of things. We simply happened to be born in this particular universe which has generated life with its particular characteristics.

Life is not perfect, and evolution is full of blunders and inauspicious beginnings. The fact that our cycle of life does not coincide with the requirements of life in the long run, the fact that we happened to be born into a civilization that is death-ridden, should not worry us too much: like fallen leaves, we shall nourish the ground which will give rise to more conducive forms of life, to more intelligent human beings, to more enhancing societies. For life will prevail And, within it, fragments and aspects of us.

In the words of the Prasna Upanishad:

'Be favorable unto us, o Life, with that invisible form of thine which is in the voice, the eye, and the ear, and which lives in the mind. Go not from us.

As a mother her child, protect us, o Life: give us glory and give us wisdom.'

NOTE

1. Although Gregory Bateson hints at epistemology of life and talks about it in his *Mind and Nature*, 1979, he does not provide one. Some of his ideas are constructive, however.